CARANGELO v. CONNECTICUT

*A Case of Lifelong Opposition to
Government Protected Child Stealing*

by
LORI CARANGELO

Access Press

copyright 2016 by Lori Carangelo
revised 2018 and 2024
published by Access Press

DISCLAIMER. The author is not an attorney and this book is not intended as legal advice. It has been compiled to provide insight into the work and stories behind the litigation, legislation, and human rights advocacy in response to America's Government Protected Child Stealing Under Color of State Sealed Adoption Laws.

Printed in the United States of America

ISBN 978-0942605-36-5

DEDICATION

This book is dedicated to the many adoptee and family rights groups whose voices are finally beginning to protest "government protected child stealing" as civil rights and human rights issue, and who I hope will bring to fruition the reform efforts of all who preceded them.

ACKNOWLEDGEMENT

In Memory of Ron Frieborn, father of seven, whose love and support helped enable me to find and know my son, and to advocate for families who had been similarly unnecessarily separated as result of government protected child stealing.

contents

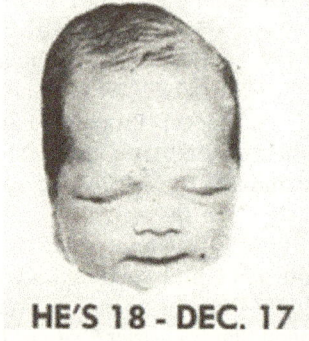

MISSING 18 YEARS!

HE'S 18 - DEC. 17

My ad that appeared in the New Haven Register Personals column, 12/15/86

Thomas William Schafrick, birth name Richard "Ricky" Marotti, at age 18,
and Lori Carangelo
Mother and Son Reunion, Mother's Day, May 10, 1987

PREFACE:
Coverup of the Coverups

The case that began in the U.S. District Court of Connecticut at New Haven in 1990, as Carangelo v. O'Neill, State of Connecticut, et al, was neither won nor lost. After arguing the case for 4 years in U.S. District Court at New Haven, Connecticut, it finally reached the United States Supreme Court. A conservative Justice's corporate law clerk, Eric C. Nelson, decided not to allow the Supreme Court to hear the case that was claiming *"government protected child stealing under color of state sealed adoption records law"* and instead threw it to the **state legislatures** despite that U.S. District Court Judge Ellen Bree Burns had already agreed that we presented "an important *federal* **question"** that also satisfied *federal* **jurisdiction.** Further, Judge Burns agreed that **"the state would be prejudiced in a case against the state if filed in a *state* court."** But also, the states have not uniformly addressed the *civil rights* of adoptees *as persons*, but rather "ownership" of adoptees as "property." Attorneys later speculated that the Supreme Court was *"not ready"* to address adoption itself as a "civil rights issue," or that they feared all past adoptions would then be void.

The idea that our United States government is complicit in literally *stealing* children also did not sit well with the general public and had divided adoption activists as being perceived as either "pro-adoption" or "anti-adoption" – until 2018 when it was widely publicized that migrant "children in cages" were not only separated from their families but also were "disappearing" – transported to undisclosed locations around the country, with no family reunification plan, hidden in foster homes, some probably sex trafficked, many alleged forcibly adopted by strangers. Shocking? Consider that half the United States population has had an adoption or relinquishment for adoption in their immediate family, and that most often the separation was financially motivated. Just as it took many court cases to end slavery, it may take many court cases to dismantle the corrupt Child Welfare and Adoption Industry. So it is important to know what cases preceded them... and to follow the dollars. That's the purpose of this book and why actual documents in the case are included here to support every word.

This book not only explains how and why my own child was "legally" stolen in 1969 for unintended, permanent sealed adoption when I had only sought temporary care and medical help for him. This book also explains how and why government protected child stealing has *escalated*. In 1969, Connecticut had no *statutory* time period for revocation of a Consent to Relinquish of Parental Rights, as California and other states did, regardless whether the Relinquishment was illegally obtained. Today, birth parents can reverse the Relinquishment in Connecticut before the adoption is finalized; however, the court will only entertain their case if it can be proven to be in the best interest of the child to return them to their birth family. Different judges may handle this situation differently. *It is relatively rare that adoption is overturned* unless it can be proven that for one reason or another the adoptive parents are not fit to parent any child.

And it caused me to focus the rest of my life on lobbying, suing, and writing, to expose the extent of government protected child stealing in order to gain support in combating it. It is also important to note two things to understand the purpose and use of this book:

(1) The United States is still the *largest market for stolen children in the world* with California being the largest U.S. market for stolen kids.

(2) The secrecy component of sealed adoption is never *requested* – It is *imposed by state law*, disguised as *"confidentiality"* and *"privacy"* but mainly protects against public awareness as to the *methods of procuring* infants and children – not only in the 1960s "Baby Scoop" era, but also now that foster care and adoption are a *multi-billion dollar industry* in which *everyone* makes money and the child is the biggest loser.

In 1990, my then-21-year old son, Tom, and I were granted a court appointed pro bono attorney. I don't think Tom, fully understood the dynamics at play when I lost him to unintended sealed adoption, nor why I regarded the practice of sealed adoption as being motivated by *financial and political gain,* even though he told me his adoptive parents "paid only $400 in legal fees" to adopt him. And *they* certainly didn't *"kidnap"* him. At the time, I didn't yet know *how* or *to whom* the cash actually flowed.

Six months after our court appointed attorney, Robert E. Grant, a law professor at Yale, amended our Class Action Complaint, he suddenly dropped out, citing *"conflict of interest."* And 200 attorneys who I solicited, nationwide, similarly claimed *"conflict of interest"* since most attorneys are involved to some extent in foster care or adoption – or with agency insurers as Grant was. And so we had to argue our case "in pro per" – and did, for four years – my son, as my co-plaintiff, present at hearings in the U.S. District Court in New Haven, Connecticut, while I was teleconferenced in from my home in Palm Desert, California.

Neither of us knew the *full scope* of what secret adoptions covered up, not only in Connecticut but nationwide, nor the powder keg that the case could ignite. Nor had my son ever actually *talked* with me about the case, or his feelings about his adoption. What my son, or any adopted child or adult may grasp *intellectually* can be light years away from dealing with it *emotionally*. He once told me that although he was happy that I had searched and found him, he took the side of sealed records advocates, saying that if he had found me instead, he would have hidden himself to just see what I looked like, failing to grasp that my sole purpose in living had been to find him. I believe that came from his and other adoptive mothers' fears of having the birth mother reclaim her child. At one point, my son reacted to my "open records" activism, saying he felt that I saw him only as "the son I lost to adoption," rather than just Tom who regards me as his "friend" because he already had a "Mom" named Lois Schafrick. His "Mom," despite being initially receptive to the reunion, evidently hoped it would be a one-time meeting. So when Tom and I were frequently flying cross country to maintain contact, she wasn't going to risk any sort of relationship *with me, or even meet me,* lest I be "real" and spoil the *"as born to"* myth that adoption agencies sell to adopters. But Tom said "Mom" didn't mind that he *continued* to be part of my life, because she felt that I *"owed him"* for the 18 years I had *"got away with not supporting him"* and now it was *"my turn."* That mindset must have been enough to feed the adversarial barrier that sealed adoption had built. No matter how much I invested in our relationship, emotionally and

8

financially, to provide him not just the cars and visits, and despite that I had tried so desperately unload the "birthmother guilt" from my shoulders, by doing all I could possibly do for him, eventually Tom literally divorced himself from what had been our mostly happy, although challenging, and sometimes hurtful 30-year post-adoption relationship that cost me tens of thousands of dollars that I had hoped would help mature and provide long-term *opportunities* to succeed in life. But at 18 and early 20s, he wasn't interested in higher education, long term employment, or business skills. His girlfriends, wives, and the children he fathered, in and out of marriages, were his priority, not college or steady employment to support them. I could then only advise him *"Do what you like and are good at and the money will follow."* What he liked and was good at was what I had been good at – buying and selling for profit. At various times in his life he was hired to liquidate retail stores that were going out of business, including Wards stores, leased a store of his own where he peddled auction finds, and his car sales evolved into selling school buses, trucks, tractors and industrial equipment. The trade-off was that he was always under stress to find "the next deal" – or the next "marks" (his friends and his two mothers) who would "loan" him money in order to snag the next deal, to make ends meet – money that he could not or would not repay. Money that I didn't yet know was partly paying for drug induced "highs" that he had begun experimenting with in his teens before I found him, because he hid it well.

At one point in the court case, my Discovery Motion produced evidence that one of the Defendants we were suing, The Children's Center in Hamden, Connecticut, a 100-year old foster-adoption agency, *had covered up unreported physical and sexual abuse of children in their care* – just as Penn State/Sandusky and the Catholic Church had hidden physical and sexual abuse of children. But Judge Ellen Bree Burns decided that the "right to privacy," of the (then-adult) abused children, and of the institution, exceeded the public's "right to know," so she issued a *Restraining Order* against my further disseminating the information and *sealed* that evidence, instead of ordering further investigation, while The Children's Center continued "business as usual"- *"cover-up of the cover-up."*

Prior to social media, I began to connect with others "similarly situated" (had the same legal claim) originating from having had their child stolen for profit via adoption. John Hayes (author of *"Theft By Adoption,"* an Amazon book now out of print) and I, could not have known, in 1969 nor in the years leading up to our class action case, that the same Connecticut Probate Judge, Glenn Knierim, had similarly Denied our requests to have updated family medical information about life-threatening conditions communicated to our children's adoptive parents, post-adoption. We didn't know how others' relinquishments of parental rights were being obtained. But this case, that began as a "class action," identified individuals in 9 states who were "similarly situated" in order to present the issue as a *federal* issue, not just a *state* concern, on how children were being procured for adoption and how it is covered-up *"under color of state secrecy laws."*

After four years of arguments, with *each part of the case raising issues for appeal,* the United States Supreme Court accepted our case for filing. But the Supreme Court Justices abdicated their responsibility to Eric C. Nelson, Law Clerk to Justice Clarence Thomas. Nelson's background was that of *corporate* law, and, for 20 years until Judge

Blackmun's sealed files were opened after his death, Nelson *hid* his written Opinion from us – an Opinion that ignored Judge Burns' ruling that our case belonged in *federal* court. Nelson advised that it belonged in *state* legislature, thus denying Certiorari, so the case could not be heard in the United States Supreme Court and there is no Appeal.

This book explains the cash incentives that have escalated the *"legal" kidnapping* of infants and children by Health and Human Services (HHS), Department of Social Services (DSS), Child Protective Services (CPS), private non-profit foster and adoption agencies, individual baby brokers, and family courts, due to the passing of:

- the 1974 federal Child Abuse and Prevention Act (CAPTA) – promoted by Walter Mondale;

- the 1997 Adoption and Safe Families Act (ASFA) – passed by Bill Clinton;

- Ronald Reagan's 1989 White House Memo #906627: *"The Adoption Option,"* that also put the federal government in to business of adoption; and

- the December 1992 Memorandum by Peter Pfund, U.S. State Department Legal Adviser, whose legal opinion *"legalizing" illegally procured or kidnapped children brought to the United States from other countries and adopted under state sealed records laws* and thus enabled the states, agencies, courts, and individuals *to receive funds* for kidnapping foreign kids as well.

Intended to help children and families, ASFA not only put the federal government into the business of adoption but also more blatantly terrorized and tore families apart for forced adoptions of infants and children while *financially rewarding* their kidnappers – government protected child stealing.

> "The highly praised increase in adoptions and foster children announced by the United States Department of Health and Human Services (DHHS) actually masks the *failure* of the new federal adoption law. **As it encouraged adoption, ASFA made it easier than ever *to take children from their parents just because those parents are poor*.**" (*PR Newswire,* 8-21-00)

In 2018, Democrats argued the consequences of 2018-2019 national budget cuts proposed by Republicans to "entitlement" programs such as MedicAid, yet gave billions of dollars in tax cuts to the nation's wealthiest top 10%. "Family preservation" of poor and middle class families was again under attack. Senator Bernie Sanders' August 2018 reaction was *"People will die."*

Federal funding of the Foster Care System was officially reported as costing $9.2-billion, or almost $20,000 per year per child since 2009, not including $2-billion spent on "adoption assistance" subsidies and services. Particularly disturbing is that the "kinship model" with true *biological* parents, has, for the past several decades, increasingly been replaced by the "adoption model" and *"psychological* parents" at a much higher cost than previously *successful* "family preservation" programs.

In early February of 2018, *"The Chronicle of Social Change"* reported multiple stories lauding the "Family First Prevention Services Act" that became law. It included the biggest change to the structure of child welfare *finance* since the establishment of the 1980 Title IV-E entitlement. The central feature of the bill (drafted by Senators Orin Hatch and Ron Wyden) is that the states will now be able to use funds derived from Title IV-E of the Social Security Act – the entitlement that pays for child welfare and family *preservation* – for "time limited (12-month) prevention services" aimed at preventing the use of foster care in maltreatment cases, formerly only allowable for spending on foster care placements and for assistance to adoptive families. So far, so good. But from 2016 until 2019, for states that "voluntarily elected" to participate, the government paid 50%; after 2026 the federal match for time-limited services pegged to the medical assistance percentage; if a parent fails to get to the point where the system is okay with returning the child, financial help for the kinship support network (of other relatives) of that child *is contingent on him or her entering foster care. Unchanged are the cash incentives for separating infants and children from their families.* Subsidies such as for "special needs" kids, are paid to foster families and adoptive parents, and "special needs" became easily categorized to fit the medical or psychiatric definitions for subsidies.

Most people understand the necessity for *uniform* state vital records and "open records" for adopted *adults*, but they may not know that the Uniform Laws Commission, rather than making adoption and birth records *uniformly accessible*, instead chose to recommend that adoptees' records be *uniformly sealed nationwide "for 99 years."*

The question then was whether to advocate for "reform" or "abolition." Reformist groups such as "Bastard Nation" and "Access Connecticut" lobby state legislators for *"unrestricted" adult adoptee access* to their original (non-falsified) birth certificate, but usually end up negotiating "compromise" legislation that would, for instance, allow one family member to "veto" disclosure of identities to the other party. Either approach *limits* disclosure until after the adoptee reaches "adult age" according to the legal age in the state in which their adoption records originated and/or were finalized, leaving half the United States population who have had an adoption or a relinquishment for adoption in their immediate family subject to detrimental secrecy laws for 18, 21 or more years. Despite that "nothing awful" has happened in Kansas where adoptees' birth records have always been "open."

"Anti-adoption" activists, on the other hand, favor *"abolishing* adoption" as we know it. But "anti-adoption" means different things to different people. The term "anti-adoption," when addressing the "core issue" of the *Constitutionality of adoption itself,* implies "abolishing" adoption in favor of more humane forms of child custody – such as individualized Child Guardianship, that already exists in law, or new expressions of child welfare that do not treat the child as *"property, without rights."* Australia has all but "abolished" adoption, now rarely utilized and considered a "last resort" in that country. "Anti-adoption" sentiments may accrue from "wrongful adoption" lawsuits filed by biological mothers and fathers claiming loss of parental rights resulting from coercion, duress, non-notification, and by adoptive parents who, for instance, claim illegality of the adoption or misrepresented medical or psychiatric condition of the child they adopted.

It is important to know that, historically, the courts were not receptive to "abolitionist" sentiment and were the main *defenders of slavery* – because our founding fathers had a *financial interest in slavery.* Today, the courts are among the main *defenders of adoption,* because today, more than ever, the courts have *financial incentives* to *increase* adoptions under the vague *"best interests of the child"* mantra. The courts and states also claim that *"the statutes are rationally related to the important state interest in adoption,"* not just *"enabling"* adoption, but aggressively *"promoting"* the multi-billion dollar adoption industry, turning a blind eye to "forced" adoptions, with no real oversight, no Due Process – where children are removed for profit from parents who are *not unfit* but who are economically disadvantaged – and handing them to strangers for a "better" life that no social worker can predict nor guarantee, as reports of physical and sexual abuse, re-homing, and trafficking of young adoptees has evidenced.

In 2018, under President Donald Trump's "Zero Tolerance" immigration policy, almost 3,000 immigrant families, having fled violence in Central America, were forcibly separated at the Texas border. The separated children, their whereabouts kept secret, were dispersed by DHHS to several states *with no plan for reunification with their parents.* Even after a court order *requiring* reunification by a specific deadline, about 2,000 children remained unaccounted for after the deadline, until the number of "missing" dwindled and were "assumed" placed in foster and adoptive homes.

Some of the 20,000 Adoptee/Birth Family Reunions
facilitated by Americans For Open Records (AmFOR)
nationwide volunteer search network

July 1989 – AmFOR's 4-City March in California
for Open Records and Child Welfare Reform

Chapter 1.
Government Protected Child Stealing
Under STATE LAW

1969 – Defining Moment – Losing My Son

I, like many others, have been involved with adoption reform efforts for over 30 years. The "defining moment" for me, the moment that set the course for the rest of my life – and my son's life – on an icy cold, bleak winter day in 1969, was when a 5-minute meeting with a social worker at The Children's Center in Hamden, Connecticut, for the purpose of obtaining *temporary care* for my son, resulted in my *permanent separation* from my 3-week old baby boy, as detailed in this chapter and in the Amended Complaint included in this compilation.

Lies and trickery resulted in my son's unintended adoption and compelled me to expose the truth, not just in my case but also for other parents who, like me, were never declared "unfit" to parent yet experienced *unnecessary* loss of their children… and for adoptees who don't deserve to lose families who had *not* abused nor neglected them, and who lost their basic rights as result of Government Protected Child Stealing that continues for financial and political gain, under state authority that alleges your child is "*a child of the state*" not of his parents (*parens patriae,* Hitler's doctrine).

While "whiter" appearing babies and children may still bring a higher price than darker complexioned children, *any* infant or child can bring $60,000 in a private adoption, and $80,000-$100,000 or more for *illicit* purposes including child sex trafficking. Foster care providers, caseworkers, lawyers, evaluators, courts, all receive *monthly cash in the form of state and federal subsidies* for each child taken.

Those who are "*anti*-adoption" are generally "*for*" individualized forms of child custody, such as temporary and permanent child Guardianship *with accountability*, when biological parents or relatives are unable to raise them, and are "*for*" emancipation of the child at legal age (which doesn't mean abandoning them at legal age as the Foster Care System does).

1974 – The Child Abuse and Prevention Act (CAPTA) and the Start of Child Protective Services (CPS) Kidnaps

When considering the police power bestowed to CPS, the following statistic bears repeating:

> **"68% of child protective cases do not involve child maltreatment. The largest percentage of CPS/DSS cases are** *for 'deprivation of necessities' due to poverty."*
> --Source: Cornell University study analysis.

In 1974, unknown to me, Connecticut adoption records were temporarily opened to benefit someone, but again closed. Also in 1974, Walter Mondale promoted the Child Abuse and Prevention Act (CAPTA) that began feeding massive amounts of federal funding to the states to set up programs ostensibly "to combat child abuse and neglect." From that, came Child Protective Services (CPS) as we know it today, administered by the Department of Health and Human Services (DHHS). After the bill passed, Mondale himself expressed concerns it could be *"misused" and lead states to create a "business" dealing in children..."* and in 2014 that is exactly what parents, family rights groups and watchdog organizations such as "Occupy Family Court" began protesting, demanding an end to CPS and family courts.

Brenda Scott, in her 1994 book, *"Out of Control: Who's Watching Our Child Protection Agencies?"* criticizes CPS stating:

> "The system, as it operates today, should be scrapped. If children are to be protected in their homes, and in the system, radical new guidelines must be adopted. At the core of the problem is the anti-family mindset of CPS. *Removal of children is their first resort, not the last.* With insufficient checks and balances, the system that was designed to *protect* children has become the *greatest perpetrator of harm.*"

But also, when children are in danger, CPS often fails to act. (--Source: Wikipedia: *"Child Protective Services")*

1986 – A Meeting of Like Minds

Long before I or any other vocal "anti-adoption" activists appeared on the scene, Jean Kittson Paton (1908-2002), a social worker, herself an adoptee, referred to adoption as *"colonialism."* She had her own "defining moment." It was in the early 1950s when her birth and adoption records that had always been public records at the vital records office were suddenly withheld from the almost 50-year-old woman when she asked to see her own, true original birth certificate but she had forgotten her unknown mother's full name by the time she felt she was ready to try to locate and contact her before it was too late to do so, given her mother's advancing age. In spite of that roadblock, she eventually did find her mother, and helped other adoptees to find their biological relatives, despite new "sealed records" laws that the states had begun to adopt not by a vote of the people it affects but by legislators with an agenda that had nothing to do with unasked for "privacy," "unwed mothers," nor "illegitimate" babies, but with *"expedience."* Soon after being denied her own birth certificate, Paton published the first studies of the *negative* effects to adoptive families from adoption and its secrecy component, in the 1950s via her organization, Orphan Voyage, as result of helping her fellow adoptees' search for their origins. She also wrote 2 books, *"Orphan Voyage,"* and *"The Adopted Break Silence."* And for 50 of her 93 years, Paton's pioneering studies, and her activism that continued until her death, earned her the title of "Mother" of The Open Records Movement and Anti-Adoption Movement in America." In 1986, I had the privilege of meeting Jean Paton at her log cabin home in remote Cedaredge, Colorado. There we were, "birth mother" and "adoptee," with identical views. Thereafter, for 16 years, we maintained mutually supportive contact, working for the same cause.

Jean more often did face-to-face, or phone-to-phone interviews, as well as by exchange of correspondence, with adoptees, parents, judges, legislators, and members of "The American Adoption Congress (AAC)," an organization she founded but which she said had "lost the focus" that she intended. According to Paton, (and as documented in her biography, *"Jean Paton and the Struggle for Adoption Reform,"* published after her death by E. Wayne Carp), the AAC instead became mostly a group of high-priced searchers who ultimately disrespected her for her views, refusing to include her without registration fees as Founder in one of their conferences. I, too, was "banned" from AAC participation due to my public anti-adoption views which included the suggestion that a *"conflict of interest"* exists when AAC's highly paid searchers lobbying for "compromise" legislation that imposed "conditions" limiting disclosure of identities, *while at the same time making a lucrative income from search fees, selling the adoptee and his biological family their own pre-adoption names and information.* So, like Paton, I continued to be an *independent voice,* documenting the pre- and post-adoption experiences of adoptees and their families *by completing their searches* via my national volunteer search network, Americans For Open Records (AmFOR), that I founded in 1989 – *and we did all this out-of-pocket.*

1987 – SB-1162 (Connecticut) – Conditions for Limited Access

In 1987, Connecticut Assemblyman Richard D. Tulisano, an adoptive father, along with Connecticut Representative Irene Favreau, passed an omnibus bill placing "conditions" on adult adoptees' access to records post-adoption, *thus concealing Connecticut agencies' methods for procuring and caring for children.* An adult adoptee would still need a court order (usually denied) to obtain information about himself and his biological family. There was no provision for "birth" parents seeking information about children they had relinquished for adoption, *which created the false impression that most mothers, and almost all fathers, "didn't want to be found,"* when the opposite was true.

Multiple state and private post-adoption reunion registries, with over 100,000 adoptees and so-called *"voluntarily* relinquishing parents" on their rolls, dispelled the myth that they gave up their children because they "didn't want" them:

98% of the mothers we located *wanted to be found.*

1987 – How I Found My Son

Our Amended Complaint in U.S. District Court at New Haven (included in this book) details the circumstances in which I lost and found my son. Eighteen years prior, in January 1969, I had been seeking *temporary* care for my son until I could get back on my feet, because we were both ill with Hong Kong Flu, a serious epidemic, and he seemed to have other medical problems as well. Pediatricians and emergency room physicians ignored my concern despite that my firstborn, a girl, died within 2 hours of birth from genetic defects, and they passed off my concern about his cries "not sounding right" as "new mother nerves," totally overlooking that he was born deaf with painful punctured eardrums, In 1969, The Children's Center's social worker LIED, claiming there was *"NO temporary foster care available"* at the time, but that if I signed over *"temporary custody"* it would authorize them to have their *medical* staff diagnose, care and treat him. But his deafness was discovered and cured by surgery *only after his adoption,* by a pediatrician paid by his adopters.

For 18 years, I tried to obtain information and regain my son via the agency, lawyers, courts and organizations. And for 18 years, my correspondence with The Children's Center and its attorneys had not elicited any guarantee that my son was *even actually adopted*, nor that he may be languishing in foster homes, nor that he was *even alive* and well – *because there is no follow-up once an adoption is finalized, and so little is known of most adoptees' outcomes.*   Irene Baker, then a social worker and employee of The Children's Center, wrote: ***"We have to assume no news is good news."*** So that's how they determined *"best interests of the child?"*

In the 18 years in which I searched for my son, no state or agency was obligated to provide even *"non-identifying"* social and *medical* information about the adopted child or his biological family to the adoptive parent, *nor to the adoptee* even at the adoptee's legal age. Today, as result of publicity that I and other searchers garnered on this issue, most states must provide *at least "non-identifying" information to adult adoptees* and, depending on the state, to birth parents or adoptive parents (with limitations). *But the adoptee and his adopters are without updated family medical history for 18 or 21 years or more.* In Connecticut, post-adoption medical updates were not transmittable from birth parents to adoptive parents, nor to adult adoptees, not even through an agency or court, even in life-and-death cases (until fairly recently, with limitations).

In 1986, Connecticut Probate Judge Glenn Knierim, said "No" to my request that Knierim inform my son or his adoptive parents of my *physician's letter* explaining my newly discovered, *inheritable* and *life-threatening* cardiac disorder and *inheritable* allergies to the prescription drugs commonly used to treat the condition.

When my story was publicized, Knierim's statement to media was that Connecticut statute *"did not compel him to do so."* Yale Law School Attorney, Stephen Wizner, in my behalf, then suggested that Knierim *could* do so *"as an administrative procedure."* Knierim again *refused*, again disproving that adoption is *"in child's best interests."* Only recently, I discovered that John Hayes (*"Adoption By Theft"*) had made a similar request to Judge Knierim and got the same Denial.

In 1987, I placed a small "personals" ad in the *New Haven Register* with my son's newborn photo and the caption *"Missing 18 Years"* avoiding mention of "adoption." A curious Register journalist, Chris Janis, interviewed me about it, resulting in a front page story, and then followup feature stories, about the issues that arose from my failed attempts to find my son, and my efforts to change laws that restrict post-adoption contact and communication, even in life-or-death situations.

As result of the publicity, I was put in touch with a "search underground," and asked to send $2100 cash, in Federal Express envelope, to Jane Servadio, a Connecticut nurse, as go-between. After checking with other mothers who, in desperation, had done the same thing, I sent the cash... and finally learned my son's adoptive name, Tom, and his whereabouts. Out of courtesy to the woman who raised him, before contacting Tom, I cleared it with her, and agreed to her request to wait until she could take him to The Children's Center "to verify that I was his mother," since the Center would likely honor an *adoptive parent's* request to review his file, once contact occurred, but not a birth parent or adoptee's similar request. On May 10, 1987, which happened to be Mother's Day, I was finally talking with my 18-year old son by phone for the first time.

The Amended Complaint alleges I applied for Welfare benefits from the Town of Hamden, yet *I never directly or knowingly applied for, signed for, nor received, Welfare payments of any kind, not even medical assistance that I WAS seeking for my son.* What actually happened was that, unknown to me, two months before my son was born, when I was 23 and divorced, my mother with whom I was living while awaiting the birth of my son, *secretly applied for Welfare benefits to be paid directly to HER*–benefits that amounted to only $76 per month – allegedly for my "rent" as her "dependent." The fact that my mother was able, under the law at the time, to apply for Welfare *without my permission or signature,* by alleging I was a "dependent child," also allegedly justified The Children's Center considering me to *be "a burden to taxpayers."*

My mother was aware that I planned to move back to California with my son as soon as he was born, because in California, I never had a problem finding work, whereas the Connecticut job market at the time my son was born limited women to either teaching (if I'd had a college degree, which I did not) or factory work, which I tried but didn't have the stamina for repetitive assembly-line work. In fact, in the years following my son's birth, I held secretarial and administrative positions in city and county government in California, was also self-employed as a secretarial service, was licensed for California Residential Real Estate Sales, had a successful business buying-restoring-and-selling over 100 cars from home, *and could have raised my son without assistance.*

Without a statutory period for Revocation of Relinquishment of Parental Rights in Connecticut, and having been denied a copy of the Relinquishment, and denied my son's original and amended (i.e. falsified) birth certificate(s) that were sealed in my son's adoption file, I could not successfully attack their "validity" in court. As far as The Children's Center, and all the attorneys I consulted over the next 18 years were concerned, it was a *"done deal."* The "protection" of secrecy, I discovered, was actually to prevent my son or his adoptive parents from knowing *he already had a mother who loved and wanted him*, **and to make it impossible to hold an agency accountable.**

Today, state and federal subsidies and other funding is received by private non-profit foster-adoption agencies if they meet a "quota," *so the more adoption placements, the more money and job security.*

1989 – AmFOR's "Repeal" Proposal to State Legislators

In 1989, when I founded Americans For Open Records (AmFOR), a national network of volunteers who assisted searches out of pocket, AmFOR's network included adoptees, parents, social workers, and some adopters who supported adoptees' and parents' "right to know." The first edition of AmFOR's newsletter, *"The Open Record,"* January-February 1989, announced our initial nationwide lobby effort for total "Repeal" of state sealed records laws. In every state, it's a crime to falsify a vital record *"as if true"* yet adoptees' "amended" birth certificates usually identify adoptive parents "as if the biological parents on date of birth," even though they didn't become "adoptive parents" until days, weeks, months or years after the birth. The true birth certificate is sealed in the court file. Although Jean Paton and I had supporters, we continued to experience the same backlash for our efforts.

On AmFOR's letterhead, which listed AmFOR's "Advisory Board" and "Liason" groups *by their permission*, I proposed a draft bill to *"Repeal"* sealed adoption records statutes – a proposal sent to hand-picked legislators in every state. Some American Adoption Congress (AAC) members DID *authorize* their inclusion, but they then distanced themselves from AmFOR due to the "anti-adoption" stigma attached to the word "repeal," even claiming that they "never gave permission" to list them on AmFOR's letterhead for mail-out of the Proposal. Paton then made it clear to the dissenters, particularly Kate Burke who headed the American Adoption Congress (AAC), that she had given me her *written permission* for inclusion.

AmFOR

Americans for Open Records • P.O. BOX 401 • PALM DESERT, CA 92261   (619) 340-26...

LORI CARANGELO
Executive Director
California Chair, ALARM Network

ADVISORY BOARD

Sharon Kaplan, BSW, MS
Director
Parenting Resources
Co-Author *Cooperative Adoption*
Tustin, California

Hope Marindin,
Executive Director
Committee for Single Adoptive
Parents
Chevy Chase, Maryland

Sandy Musser,
National Chairperson
ALARM (Advocating Legislation
for Reform Movement)
Author *I Would Have Searched
Forever*
Cape Coral, Florida

Bruce M. Rappeport,
Executive Director
Independent Adoption Center
Pleasant Hill, California

Jon R. Ryan, *President*
NOBAR (National Organization of
Birthfathers and Adoption Reform)
Baltimore, Maryland

Dorothy Thurriage, *Director*
Search Finders of California, and
Doreen Alegrete, *Co-Director*
PAST (Professional Adoption Search
Team)
Certified National Search
Consultants
San Jose, California

CANADA

Judith Kizell Brans, *President*
Parent Finders—National Capital
Region
Ottawa, Ontario

LIAISON

AAC (American Adoption
Congress)
Hal Aigner, Journalist
Author *Adoption in America
Coming of Age*
ALMA (Adoptees' Liberty
Movement Assn.)
APFOR (Adoptive Parents for
Open Records)
CUB (Concerned United Birthparents)
Nancy L. Fisher, MD, MPH
Society of Human Genetics
ISRR (International Sounders
Reunion Registry)
National Adoption Search Hotline
National Council on
Children's Rights
Leah Pienatalier, MSW
Catholic Social Service
(Open Adoption)
Carol Stack, Ph.D., Director
Center for the Study of the Family and
the State—Duke University

January 1, 1989 (by return-receipt mail)

RE: ENCLOSED BILL PROPOSAL TO REPEAL
YOUR STATE'S LAW(S) PERTAINING TO
FALSIFYING AND SEALING OF BIRTH RECORDS
IN INFANT AND CHILD ADOPTIONS.

FISCAL IMPACT: -0-
Saves State expenses of
intermediary disclosure.

Moral issues always preclude compromise. Opening adoption
records is certainly one of those issues. The public interest
is always a more compelling reason for reform than is any
individual's right to privacy.

The enclosed Bill Proposal is a historic piece of proposed
legislation which you, for a total of 50 states'(& Wash.,D.C.)
legislators will be introducing, simultaneously, in 1989.
(See enclosed roster of those legislators, by state.) Much
supporting documentation accompanies this proposal and our
representatives and liaison in each state will work with you
on drafting, supporting, and expediting this Bill for 1989.
AmFOR represents more than 135,000,000 Americans affected
by adoption secrecy (see enclosed analysis), and more than
800 national organizations favoring Repeal.

"Compromise legislation," such as adult mutual consent
registries, or adult access to unfalsified records, has
proven unsatisfactory to the needs and rights of parties
known as the "adoption triad," particularly of the minor
adoptee who, for 18-21 years or more is injured by the
same sealed records laws which ostensibly were enacted
"in the best interests of the child." Injury includes
medical, psychiatric, emotional and criminal exploitation
of and by the Adopted Americans and the System. (See AmFOR
brochure and "Adoption Issues Stats-At-A-Glance" -yellow sheet)

The 1960's-70's student anti-war/civil rights demonstrations,
the women's movement, environmentalism, among many other
diverse causes, opened up "closed" systems. 1989 is
The Year Of The Adopted American Revolution, creating with
a planned April 22 March On Washington. The sealed adoption
record is unConstitutional and unAmerican as it discriminates
against those who did not request its "protection." Please
inform us as to your needs and progress on this Bill which
cannot wait another year.

Respectfully,

Lori Carangelo
LORI CARANGELO, National Chairperson

ADOPTEE RIGHTS ARE HUMAN RIGHTS

"A right is not a right, in America, unless it extends to all Americans."
—Special Watergate Prosecutor Archibald Cox

According to E. Wayne Carp, Jean Paton's biographer, Paton *"praised what Carangelo's group had proposed, for 'having as much substance on one page as any single page I have seen,'"* and Paton suggested to Kate Burke that AAC should open its Board to people who acted independently from the organization. Paton added that she herself had always welcomed liaisons *"such as Carangelo who was hitting the nail with the hammer."* Burke, an adoptee whose "birth" mother initially stalled off meeting for 3 years, responded 2 months later and *"was defensive and acerbic... accusing Carangelo's literature as being filled with wrong information–and flat out lies"* because I did not follow the party line. Years later, Access Connecticut submitted a bill proposal for unrestricted Connecticut *adult* adoptee access to their original birth certificate requiring *"repeal"* of part of the existing statute.

1989-2012 – AmFOR and ALARM: That "Small Noisey Group" Lobbying and Circumventing Law and the System

I also joined forces with the organization, Advocating Legislation for Adoption Reform (ALARM), founded by Sandra K. Musser of Florida. Any gains AmFOR and ALARM made as "sister organizations" were constantly threatened with reversal by the well-funded National Committee For Adoption (NCFA), renamed National Council For Adoption, then-headed by its Director, Bill Pierce, as a lobby arm of Christian adoption agencies, spouting lies and half-truths. It was revealed in Pierce's files released after his death that Pierce constantly monitored AmFOR and ALARM's activities, indicating his concern about the growing influence of what he called out *"small noisy group."*

We proved to ourselves, over and over again, the futility of the justice system when I and others took adoptees and birth parents to Los Angeles and Orange County courts to help them communicate in terms of required "good cause" for disclosure from their sealed adoption files to the persons named in those files. They were always Denied – not just James Grant George, a 48-year old *Missouri* adoptee who needed a bone marrow transplant from a willing blood relative to save his life, but also Virgie Byrns, the *dying* woman I brought before a *Los Angeles* judge who refused to allow her to tell her son she loved him before she died. Fortunately, I was able to identify and locate her son anyhow (as detailed in the Orange County Register article on page 34). The system has no idea what was *"in the best interests"* of adoptees and *didn't want to know*.

Getting nowhere in the *State courts*, I lobbied *State legislators* as "Americans For Open Records (AmFOR)," and staged demonstrations via a "March on Sacramento," that included AmFOR's entry of a parade float with our "open records" banner in a July 4th Independence Day parade, joined by peaceful protester groups against sealed records including "Mothers and Others for Peace," "National Association of State VOCAL Organizations (NASVO)," and I also joined forces with Jon Ryan's "National Organization of Birthfathers And Reform (NOBAR)" supporting their lawsuits against baby brokers circumventing fathers who were asserting their parental rights.

22

Sandy Musser, aka ALARM and I "divided up" the states in which our respective members would be vigilant to inform all about pending adoption legislation – Sandy resided in Florida and so kept tabs on adoption and family welfare legislation in states "East of the Mississippi." Since I resided in California, I monitored and reported on such legislation in states "West of the Mississippi" and found that significant adoption-related proposals were hidden in unrelated bills. We would notify each other's networks about bills of interest, and our members would answer the call to "support" or "oppose" bills they would otherwise not have been aware of – for example:

- **Michigan-SB-114, SB-115**, "Adult access to records" which AmFOR *supported* (9-31-91);

- **Michigan-SB-1638** – Seeking *$50-Million Appropriation to Promote Adoption*. AmFOR **opposed** it. My "open letter" published in the *Vassar (MI) PioneerTimes,* 8-12-98, helped DEFEAT this bill (MI Senator Spencer Abraham, 7-22-98);

- **Nebraska-LB-495** – Prohibiting "Baby Want-Ads" by baby brokers – which AmFOR *supported* and also voiced opposition to similar proposals in California;

- **Oregon-1998 Ballot Measure 58** – Funded by an adoptee Helen Hill from her $100,000 inheritance, it sought adult adoptee access to original birth certificate without court order, by showing ID. The effort was *supported* by AmFOR & ALARM and PASSED by 609,268 voters in 1998, with 454,122 voters against it; went into effect in Y-2000 after court challenges; in 2014 a law was PASSED permitting adult adoptees AND their "birth" parents access to the court's adoption file with ID + $25 and copy fee.

- **California-AB-548** "Priority in Placement" in foster and adoption placements for family preservation *supported* by AmFOR, PASSED; (Assemblywoman Gwen Moore, 2-16-90).

- **California-AB-3907** – Adult Access to Adoption Records – which DID NOT PASS although re-submitted in the next session as AB-1444 (pertaining to "adult adoptee access), and AB-1447 (pertaining to "birth" parents); AmFOR, Eugene Austin, a long-time fathers' rights activist who "reverse kidnapped" children at gunpoint across state lines and returned them to the parent holding the custody order in divorce cases, and he was a prolific writer – and Mary Foess, *Bonding by Blood Unlimited* – were vocal *supporters*, but it DID NOT PASS. (Assemblyman Charles Quackenbush, an adopter, 3-23-90)

- **California-AB-3504** – When *"The Adoption Option"* was promoted in Schools, AmFOR, with AARM, ACLU, American Association of University Women (AAUW), and Planned Parenthood *opposed* it; my article about it was published in the *Los Angeles Times* and helped DEFEAT this bill initiated by baby broker Bruce Rappaport (Assemblyman Mountjoy and Theresa Hughes, Chair, California Committee on Health, Education & Welfare, 4-5-90)

- **California-CB-531**, Make Open Adoption Agreements "Enforceable" in California – AmFOR *supported* the bill; PASSED. (Rasmussen, California Department of Health and Human Services, 2-5-93)

By changing its name from "National *Committee* For Adoption to "National *Council* For Adoption," NCFA, appeared to be a "government agency" which it is not. And by appearing governmental, NCFA was able to propagandize adoption to the general public with ads touting "happy, successful adoptees," using a few birth mothers demanding "anonymity" at very "public" legislative hearings. One of NCFA's underhanded methods of operation included enlisting a clique of propagandists who monitored online adoption topic chat forums 24/7, and would immediately circle the wagons to "neutralize" anyone engaging in politically incorrect *"anti-adoption"* dialogue, by bullying, heckling, ridiculing, antagonizing, hacking, libeling, and other "dirty tricks" designed to try to intimidate and/or discredit us in much the same way that former President Trump smears his opposition. At one point, NCFA minions hacked AmFOR's website, changing portions to read the opposite of the original message, later claiming the criminal violation was "just a parody."

NCFA also persuaded corporate leaders such as Wendy's founder, Dave Thomas, an orphan *who always knew his mother and so did not share the sealed adoption experience*, to be their "poster child" promoting the *"successful adoptee"* pitch to a succession of United States presidents, beginning with Ronald Reagan.

In 1989, President Ronald Reagan blindly bought NCFA's rhetoric and skewed statistics, and, in turn, convinced the masses to blindly fund Reagan's White House Memo #906627: *"The Adoption Option"* of July 24, 1989. Thus, the *federal* government which has always deflected complaints about adoption violating Due Process and basic civil rights, by calling any adoption issue a *"state* matter," was suddenly in the adoption business – by paying *federal* subsidies to states, adopters, agencies, lawyers, courts and anyone who helps facilitate "more" adoptions. Meanwhile, Reagan's adopted son, Michael, wrote of his feeling treated as an "outsider" in his adoptive family (in his book, *"On the Outside Looking In"*).

At some point there was a "rift" between Sandy Musser and me. I believe Sandy, a paid searcher, took it personally when I publicly questioned the *"conflict of interest"* presented by the American Adoption Congress (AAC), an umbrella of highly paid search groups, like Sandy's, at the same time lobbying for *"compromise legislation"* regarding records access, while AmFOR's network of searchers demonstrated it was possible to solve many searches *without fees*, just more difficult and not as lucrative.
Jean Paton also deplored the fact that adoption-affected people were extorting their fellow adoptees and parents.

When it was revealed that the average income derived from such search businesses was $60,000 per year, I repeated that claim during a radio talk show about finding families, in which Kate Burke of AAC, and my son and I, were patched in from our homes at opposite sides of the country, answering questions from callers. When I mentioned the "$60,000 a year search businesses," the deafening silence was as though the station had blown a fuse, and it took awhile before Burke regained her composure and responded that she "didn't know of anyone who made $60,000 a year *consistently,*" thus confirming that some *do* make that amount, even if "not inconsistently."

Social workers employed by an agency holding an adoption file and who charge for being a "Confidential Intermediary (CI)" also have a "conflict of interest" in that they have the "discretion" to *summarize or withhold* information in the interest of protecting the agency from scrutiny or lawsuit.

When I tried to assist an *incarcerated* Michigan adoptee, Greg Mox, to obtain at least his *"non-identifying* information" from Catholic Social Services of Macomb, which information may include any *"non-identifying family medical information to which he was then entitled under Michigan law,* after another incarcerated Michigan adoptee had obtained *his* non-ID from Catholic Social Services in a different Michigan county, Sister Joanne Ales voiced her bias against prisoners in general. She refused to accept proof of Greg Mox's indigent prisoner status, nor waive her $60 fee. Instead she offered, as Confidential Intermediary, to do a "search" for Greg's mother for $250. I pointed out to her, if the prisoner doesn't have $60 he's not likely to be able come up with $250, to which she responded, *"Prisoners can get the money."* But even if he could pay, the deck was stacked against Greg Mox getting anything for his money since there is "no guarantee" of accuracy or even provision of anything. Greg's crime? He murdered his adoptive parents who he saw (in his words) as *"trying to make him grow into the skin of the biological child they could not have,"* and preventing him discovering his origins.

The reunions accomplished by search groups, and what they disclosed, became a testament to the need for open records legislation. But "the means" by which searches were accomplished varied and is what would get Sandy Musser into trouble with the law. On July 30, 1993, the *New York Times* reported that Musser, who was *"charging $450 to $2500 or more for successful searches,"* and who stated she had facilitated "500 searches from 1977 to 1993," was arrested in a sting operation by the FBI. Although it was her paid searcher, Barbara Moskowitz, who committed the crime of "gaining access to confidential Social Security and medical records by using various ruses," Sandy, as head of the organization employing Moskowitz, was "found guilty of conspiring with Barbara Moskowitz, a Cleveland researcher" as an "adoption genealogist" who gained access "to confidential information" *across state lines* – so federal jurisdiction applied. In a plea bargain, Musser chose to spend 4 months in jail, rather than pay a hefty fine, to become a martyr for open records in her book *"To Prison With Love"* detailing her case.

Even though Sandy and I had our differences, I, like others, wrote support letters for her while she was in jail. We were both mothers who had unjustly lost our children to

25

adoption. That, and our mutual respect of each other's intense dedication to dismantling the corrupt system, took precedence. But Kate Burke, and other former friends of Sandy Musser's, then distanced themselves from her, just as they had distanced themselves from AmFOR and Jean Paton.

1997 – HR-867 the Federal Adoption and Safe Families Act (ASFA)

In 1997 The Adoption and Safe Families Act (ASFA) was passed by President Bill Clinton. The public relations campaign promoted it as "a way to help abused and neglected children who languished in Foster Care for years, often being shuffled among dozens of foster homes, never having a real home and family." The drive of the ASFA initiative is the offer of cash as "*adoption incentive bonuses*" to states for every child they adopt out of foster care with the goal of *doubling adoptions by 2002 and sustaining that for each subsequent year*. An interesting point is that the Cape Cod and Islands office "led the state" in terms of processing kids into the system and having them adopted out – more than *inner city* areas including housing projects such as Mission Hill, Brockton, Lynn, etc. It was apparent that a whole new industry was put into motion *with a sweet marketing scheme that even Bill Gates could envy*. Accompanying ASFA, Clinton requested by Executive Memorandum an initiative entitled "Adoption 2002" to be implemented and managed by DHHS *while Hilary Clinton aggressively advocated for adoption*. The initiative not only gives adoption bonuses to the states, it also provides cash subsidies to adopters until the child turns 18, and *everyone makes money from separating children from their biological families*. The fact that this program was run by DHHS, as ordered from the very top, explains why citizens who are victims of the Department of Social Services (DSS) get no response from their legislators. And it explains why no one in the Administration cared about the abuse and fatalities of children in the "care" of DSS and why no one wants to hear about the broken arms, verbal abuse, or rapes. ***They are just "business casualties."***

The way the adoption bonuses have worked is that each state is given a baseline number of "*expected adoptions based on population.*" For every child that DSS can adopt out, there's a bonus of $4,000 to $6,000. But that is just the *starting figure* in a complex mathematical formula. Each bonus is MULTIPLIED by the percentage that the state has managed to exceed its baseline adoption number. The states must then maintain this increased baseline in each successive year. Seizing upon this excellent tool for marketing adoption, the North American Council on adoptable Children (NACAC) set up a program called "National Adoption Assistance Training, Resources and Information Network (NAATRIN)." The "Technical Assistance" section supports:

- the goal of encouraging more adoptions out of the foster care system;
- the development of best practice guidelines for ***expediting*** the termination of parental rights;
- the development of special units and expertise in moving children toward adoption as a permanent goal;
- models to encourage the ***fast tracking*** of children who have not attained one year of age into pre-adoptive placements; and

26

- the development of programs that place children into pre-adoptive placements *without waiting for termination of parental rights.*

Some of the other incentives offered are "innovative grants" to reduce barriers to adoption [i.e., the parents], more state support for adoptive families (rather than financial help for biological family preservation), and making adoption more affordable by providing cash subsidies and tax credits.

Clinton further directed DHHS to develop an Internet website to "link the children in Foster Care with adoptive families." If you don't find anything you like by "window shopping" the government's website, you can surf over to "AdoptShoppe." If you prefer to "kick the tires" instead of just looking at photos, there's a DSS "Adoption Fair" where live children are put on display for all to walk around and browse – *like a flea market that sells kids.* After an adoption is finalized, adopters can collect cash subsidies until the child is 18, or if the child stays in school, subsidies continue until age 22. There are also state funded subsidies which then ranged from $410-$486 per month, as well as other kinds of federal funding through a Title IV-E section of the Social Security Act for children who can be designated as having "special needs," which, of course, they all can. "Special needs," according to NAATRIN State Subsidy Profile, can be defined as:
- physical disability;
- mental disability;
- emotional disturbance;
- a significant emotional tie with the Foster Parents where the child had resided with Foster Parents for one or more years.
- [But their "significant emotional ties with their biological families since birth never enter the equation];
- a child 12 years of age or older;
- racial or ethnic factors;
- child having siblings or half siblings.

"Special needs" children may also get an additional Social Security check; adopters also receive Medicaid for the child, a clothing allowance, as well as reimbursement of adoption costs such as adoption fees, court and attorney fees, cost of the adoption home study, and "reasonable costs of food and lodging for the child and adopters when necessary to complete the adoption process." In their report on *"State of the Children,"* Boston's Institute for Children states: "In part because the states can garner extra federal funds for 'special needs children, *the 'special need' designation had been broadened so far as to become meaningless."* Under Title XX of the Social Security Act, adopters are also entitled to "Post-Adoption Services" that can be helpful in keeping adoptive families intact, including:
- daycare;
- specialized daycare;
- respite care;
- in-house support services such as housekeeping;
- personal care, counseling and other child welfare services

An example of the *"cash for kids"* mentality is evident in the following, posted online by a Florida adopter:

> *"We receive a subsidy of $1900 from the state of Florida and are*
> *trying to adopt 3 more teens as we will get subsidies for them too."*
> --Source: Nev Moore, in "Adoption Bonuses: The Money
> Behind the Madness," Massachusetts News, 1-20-14)

And the kicker is that the regulations allege "adoption assistance is based solely on the needs of the child *without regard to the income of the [adoptive] family."* In other words, adopters can avail themselves of the kinds of services *denied* to biological families labeled *"economically unfit to parent."* Adopters and Foster Parents were not subjected to psychological evaluations, inkblot tests, MMPIs, drug and alcohol evaluations, or urine screens, as the natural parents were.

Winter 2003, the last issue of *"The Open Record"* was published, and all back issues were archived on AmFOR's website, later on Facebook, for public access. From 1989 until 2009 about 20,000 adoptee-parent reunions were facilitated by AmFOR including for an increasing number of *incarcerated* adoptees whose "birth" parents agreed to varying degrees of contact and/or help. Several of their stories were detailed in annually updated editions of *"Chosen Children."*

In 2012, the "Child Abuse Prevention and Treatment Act (CAPTA) of 1974" was bolstered with money incentives that also increased *false* claims of child abuse and *forced* adoption placements – more government protected child stealing.

As of 2019, in Connecticut, adoptees whose adoptions were finalized on or after October 1, 1983 may access their original birth certificate on request with an application and $15 fee to the Department of Children and Families "counseling"; other adult adoptees desiring disclosure must obtain a court order for a Confidential Intermediary (CI) and/or be matched on the state's reunion registry if both parties have filed a Waiver of Confidentiality and consent to disclosure.

JOSEPH PALADINO, M.D.
FAMILY PRACTICE AND GERIATRICS
73-255 EL PASEO, SUITE 4
PALM DESERT, CA. 92260

TELEPHONE (619) 340-1301

March 2, 1987

Judge Glenn Knierim
c/o Jean Watson
Probate Administration
186 Newington Road
West Hartford, Connecticut

RE: Lori Carangelo (formerly Lorraine Marotti-Konzal), birth-mother of Richard
Anthony Marotti (child born 12/17/68; placed with adoptive parents 2/6/69)

Dear Judge Knierim and Ms. Watson:

I have reviewed Mrs. Carangelo's medical records. I agree with her previous physician's
(Dr. Robert Bernstein's) diagnosis of cardiac mitral valve prolapse that is a permanent
potentially genetically transmitted condition, and to request that this information
contained herein be communicated to the adoptive parents of Ms. Carangelo's son, along
with Ms. Carengelo's request that she be contacted by her son. Ms. Carangelo's history
of cardiac arrhythmia and syncope can be life-threatening particularily as she has a
history of allergy and adverse reactions to at least 10 cardiac medications traditionally
prescribed to control such arrhythmia. Drug allergies may also be genetically transmitted.

Sincerely,

JOSEPH PALADINO, M.D.

JP:dkh

Letter from Dr. Paladino to CT Judge Glenn Knierim, 3/2/87

New Haven Register

SERVING CONNECTICUT SINCE 1812

NEW HAVEN, CONN., 06511, MONDAY, DECEMBER 15, 1986

Mom hopes ad will end adoption mystery

By Chris Janis
Staff Reporter

The Sunday newspaper notice read: "Missing 18 years!"

Under it was a clipped photograph of a sleeping newborn boy — a picture taken almost 18 years ago at the Hospital of St. Raphael. Under that was another line.

He will be 18 Wednesday, the ad says.

With that 4¼- by 3¾-inch advertisement, former Hamden resident Lorraine Carangelo began her public search Sunday for a child that she says she bore a long time ago. She knew him for only two weeks before placing him for adoption.

"This is something I have kept with me for 18 years and maybe he has too," Carangelo, a cookbook publisher now living in Palm Desert, Calif., said in a telephone interview Sunday.

"I would do anything I could for him. If he wanted, I would fly him out here to talk or I would go back (to Connecticut). Just so he would know. I don't want to upset his adoptive parents."

Carangelo, 41, said she is forbidden by law to initiate a search for her child, but she is hoping that since her son — born Richard Anthony Marotti — will be 18 years old and legally considered an adult, he will ask to find her.

Under state statutes, a parent who gives up a child for adoption gives up all rights to the child and cannot legally search for it. The law also says adults who were adopted as children can apply in person for information concerning their biological parents.

They can apply through the courts or the department or agency through which they were adopted.

Carangelo said she gave her baby to the Children's Center in Hamden, a private adoption agency serving Greater New Haven.

The information includes the age of the parents at the birth, health, physical appearance, education, reasons for adoption, religion, health history, talents and hobbies of the biological parent.

The identity of the biological parents can be made available to the adoptee if the biological parents consent and if a judge deems the information would not be di

See Adoption page 2

MISSING 18 YEARS!

HE'S 18 - DEC. 17

Portion of advertisement appearing in Sunday's Register.

Adoption: Mother tries to end 18-year mystery

Continued from page 1

ruptive to the adoptive person or the biological parents.

"I have been waiting years to do this," she said. "I have reams of correspondence of all the attempts I've made in other ways to make contact with the (adoptive) parents. I tried through the courts and the Children's Center. I even wrote letters to the editor."

Carangelo's ad stated that her baby was placed in adoption around January 1969, "through a bizarre set of circumstances." She said she was divorced when she became pregnant.

Carangelo said that she and the baby had been very ill after the birth.

"He was 2 weeks old with a digestive problem. He cried incessantly and didn't digest food properly," she said.

"I asked for foster care at the Children's Center in Hamden and was told there was no foster care. I was told he would have to be given up for adoption. I did relinquish him legally, but I did not want to give him up. I thought I could give the baby up and then get it back when I was better. In my mind, I thought all it would take was a lawyer."

"It has always been the policy of the children's center to provide foster care for babies whose mothers have felt at birth that they cannot take care of them," Rosario Caicedo, a social worker at the center, said today.

Carangelo said she previously had lost a child at birth and has children now.

"There was no way until he was 18 to open up his record," she continued. "He's 18 now and I don't want to disrupt his life, but from all the adoptees I have talked with, they all seem to know they are adopted."

Carangelo said she lived in Hamden until she graduated from high school in 1963 and moved to California. She said she married in New Haven in 1967, was divorced in 1968, became pregnant after she was divorced and came back to Connecticut to have the baby. After the baby was adopted, she said, she went back to California.

"I assume he is in the area and has a nice home and family," she said. "I want to satisfy his need to know as well as my need to know that he is alive and well."

A staff member at the Children's Center this morning confirmed the agency handled the Marotti adoption.

Carangelo asks that anyone who may have recognized the photograph in Sunday's Register, or who knows an adopted boy who will be 18 years old Thursday contact her at (619) 346-4729 or Box 3023, Palm Desert, Calif. 92261.

30

Mother's 18-year search ends

Son given up for adoption is located in Connecticut

By ANTHONY BORDERS
The Press-Enterprise

Mother's Day, a crowded Dallas airport terminal and Lori Carangelo is trembling as she dials a phone.

She is calling her son, whom she has neither seen nor heard from for 18 years.

She remembers him only as 3-week-old Richard, wrapped tight against a Connecticut cold, as he was turned over to a private adoption agency. Soon thereafter, he was put up for adoption.

The Indian Wells resident thought about her son almost every day. To find him, to know what happened to him, became her passion. There were private investigators, letters to legislators, newspaper stories and advertisements, the latter with a baby picture, phone number and a "Missing 18 Years" headline.

Connecticut officialdom, which held the adoption records and details of where the child might be found, under law could offer little help. That cold shoulder not only sparked Carangelo's desire to find the boy, but also a drive to change the adoption laws blocking her path.

There was no success until, "like a miracle," Carangelo used unofficial channels and help from adoption-rights groups to get her

KURT MILLER/The Press-Enterprise

Lori Carangelo with a folder of information and photograph of infant child she gave up for adoption 18 years ago. Just recently, a t enabled here to locate her son.

first significant lead. A woman called, promising information on Carangelo's son within a day.

The next day, about a week before before Mother's Day, the phone rang. A voice provided a name and a phone number in Connecticut. This, the contact said, was her son's home.

Not sure if she wasn't being led on a wild goose chase, Carangelo called. She talked quickly but carefully, explaining in detail the bizarre circumstances which led to the call out of the blue. The woman listened, Carangelo says, and wanted to know more.

"Her primary concern was that she did not want him to be hurt if this was not his mother."

Carangelo agreed to send along any information she had about her son. A firm identification had to be made before the woman would tell her 18-year-old son that his natural mother apparently had located him.

So it was that, roughly a wee later, on the way back to th desert from a previously arranged trip to Italy, Carangelo found herself standing at a Dallas airport terminal phone booth, on Mother's Day, dialing the numbe where her son worked. All she knew was that his first name is "Tommy."

The phone rang. He answered and they talked for two minutes. "I have a son, a grown son," she remembers thinking a the conversation began awkwardly. They exchanged brief biographical information.

She never had another child. She was living in the desert and writing cookbooks.

He had a job in a car wa.. in Meriden, Conn., not far from hu Hamden birthplace.

The paper chase for birth parents

Local woman seeks change in adoption rules

By CHRISTINE MAHR
and JULIE ATTAWAY
Staff writers

COACHELLA — Some kids get tagged with adoring nicknames from loving parents.

But Tami Cloo of Coachella was different.

"My father and brother would always call me the black sheep," said Cloo, 31.

"I was adopted and they made sure I knew I was different."

Cloo, born in Martinez near Berkeley, was abandoned in Riverside County when she was a few months old. She didn't learn that she was adopted until she was 7.

There was little love and affection from her adoptive parents. Her father, whom she described as abusive and an alcoholic, often beat her, she said.

She said she frequently ran away from home and ended up in "about nine or 10 foster homes," along with having to undergo psychological counseling.

This unhappy relationship with her adoptive parents recently fueled Cloo's desire to find her real mother.

Her paper chase through the California Department of Social Services, however, has been unsuccessful. State and federal laws won't let her view her original birth records.

She now has turned to the courts for help.

Cloo recently filed a lawsuit in Superior Court in Indio in an attempt to free her adoption records and receive money for the physical and psychological suffering she said resulted from her adoption.

Now a single mother and about to be married, Cloo still is determined to find her mother, even though the woman abandoned her.

"People always were telling me I didn't look like my parents so I asked them why I didn't look like them," she said. "That's when they told me I was adopted.

"I don't hold it against her that she left me," Cloo said of her natural mother. "I just want to know who she is."

Cloo is just one of millions of people nationwide who want to find their natural parents.

There are about 1,000 organizations which conduct searches for adopted children and parents who gave up their children for adoption. Membership fees range from $50 to $75, but a search could cost from $300 to several thousand dollars with little or no

MAX ORTIZ/Staff photographer

CRUSADER: Lori Carangelo helps adopted children discover their real parents. Her organiza-　Hon. called Americans for Open Records, seeks to open records to adoptees.

guarantee.

Leading a local, donation-only method is Palm Desert resident Lori Carangelo, the executive director of the Palm Desert-based Americans for Open Records, her own lobbying and educational network.

Carangelo, who's helping Cloo with her case, became a crusader for the rights of adopted children and their natural parents as a result of her own 18-year struggle to contact the son she gave up for adoption when she was a young woman.

She said she did not want to give up her child, but the infant required more intensive medical care than she could give. At the time, she was told it was the only option.

After years of frustration, she finally found her son with the aid

of a private organization that works to unite adopted children and their natural parents. The search cost her $2,500, and it was just one of many she had tried.

Carangelo founded the Americans for Open Records in January of 1989 to advise others in their search. She asks for donations because she is fighting for the issue of open adoption records, rather than specifically trying to reunite families. She is not an attorney, but she volunteers her time, experience, money and supplies.

To date, she has filed six lawsuits in two states. She is working on six other petitions for courts in two other states. She also has advised more than 2,000 people who have written her asking for suggestions and help.

Although the lawsuits may vary in the names of the players

and the states, each suit says basically the same thing — these individuals were allegedly "abandoned" or adopted without "late signed consent of their natural parents, and then denied access to sealed adoption records.

The suits allege that denying access to confidential, sealed adoption records is a violation of a person's civil rights and denial of due process.

Additionally, the suits allege that punishing a child (by sealing adoption records) for the misconduct of parents is unconstitutional.

"We have not been able to find attorneys to represent us," Carangelo said. "They just don't seem to be willing to take on the issue."

Even the American Civil Liberties Union has turned her down

See ADOPTED/H6

Continued from H1

for representation, saying it is too complicated an issue.

Routinely, states issue revised birth certificates showing the names of the adoptive parents, instead of the natural parents. The original is sealed and filed.

In California, an adoptee at least 18 years old can petition the court to unseal the original birth records — but only if the natural parents and adoptive parents agree. Many times, the natural parents have moved away.

Additionally, the petitioner must show a just cause, such as a medical emergency.

"Curiosity is not a sufficient reason for the courts," Carangelo said.

Carangelo said Riverside County adoption officials have medical re-

cords naming Cloo's natural mother. But they don't have the woman's consent, and they are not allowed by state law to search for her.

THE ORANGE COUNTY Register

April 29, 1990

Bill, suit seek to open up all adoption files

But some say privacy must remain guarded

By Carroll Lachnit
The Register

Virgie Byrns has an aging, brittle baby book and a black-and-white snapshot that shows her with an infant in her arms.

But that is all Byrns, 70, of Santa Ana has to remind her of her son, Wayne. He was placed for adoption nearly 40 years ago by her ex-husband, without her permission or knowledge, she said.

Byrns said her attempts to find her son were stymied by state laws that keep adoption records confidential. Strokes and heart disease sapped the energy she needed to fight the bureaucracy, she said.

"I tried my best to do things for myself," she said. "But I gave up."

Others have picked up the battle, however.

Americans for Open Records, an adoption civil-liberties group, has filed a class-action lawsuit on behalf of Byrns and two adult adoptees in federal court, saying the

Please see ADOPTION/10

Virgie Byrns of Santa Ana holds a baby book that has prints of her son's hands and feet on its cover. She says her child was put up for adoption in 1952 without her permission by her ex-husband.

Paul Kuroda/The Register

...te and a private adoption agencies have violated their constitutional rights by sealing their records. Besides seeking access to records, the suit is asking for $30 million in damages for the emotional distress it says has been caused by the plaintiffs' futile searches. A hearing will be held May 21 in Los Angeles to determine whether the three meet the legal requirements for being a class.

A bill that would change California's closed adoption-records law is working its way through the Assembly. If it passes, adoptive parents, adult adoptees and birth parents could easily obtain information about the other parties involved in the adoption.

Adoptees and birth parents now must prove to a judge that they have a good reason to have records unsealed. Adult adoptees must get adoptive parent's permission before the state will match their quest for information with any similar request filed by their birth parents.

Adoptees who are fed up with the system will line up at county courthouses Tuesday, demanding if judges give them access to their adoption files, said Kate Burke, president of American Adoption Congress, the organization that helped draft the open-records bill.

"Basic civil rights are being violated," she said.

At least one adoption organization is opposed to the open-records movement. The National Committee For Adoption believes that such changes violate a promise of confidentiality that states and adoption agencies give women who put their children up for adoption.

William Pierce, the committee's president, said many women specifically chose adoption because they were told that their names never would be revealed.

Pierce said the best method for birth parents and adopted children who want to find each other is to file a waiver of confidentiality, which can be done in California and 21 other states.

They can file the waiver with the state Department of Social Services or private adoption agencies. But before the state or agency will make a match and disclose names and addresses, a birth parent, an adoptive parent and an adoptee must sign the waiver.

Without the three-way confidentiality waiver, birth parents and adoptees in California can only receive non-identifying information about each other from the state or adoption agency that completed the adoption.

The information usually includes the age, occupation, background and interests of the adoptive and birth parents and notes made by social workers on how adopted children were adjusting to their new life. The information does not contain names or addresses.

Parents whose children were removed by courts after abuse or neglect are not allowed to receive even non-identifying information, Burke said.

In adoptions that were completed after 1984, a birth mother can sign a form allowing the state or agency to give her name and last known address to the child when he or she reaches age 21.

The bill to change the law, AB3907, would drop restrictions and open adoption records to adopting parents, adult adoptees and birth parents. It passed the Assembly Justice Committee on Wednesday, said Rob Lapsley, an aide to Assemblyman Chas Quackenbush, R-Saratoga, the bill's sponsor.

The solution to such a confrontation is simple, she said.

"Birth parents can say, 'No, I don't want to know you,'" she said. "What must be known is that searches (for birth parents and adopted children) are done all the time. People say no, and people respect their wishes and handle it like adults."

Pierce said the contacts are not that simple. A caller on Friday told him that she had taken great pains to keep secret her decision to give up her baby 37 years ago. But the adoptee's persistent efforts to contact her "made the last five years hell," he said.

"People have the right to be left alone," he said.

The new law would respect the wishes of birth mothers who did not sign the address form, and would not supply information that identified them, Lapsley said.

Burke said the bill might be refined later to deal with adoption records of children who were removed from their parents' custody because of abuse or neglect. She said the new law probably would not allow those parents to get information about the children, unless they could show a judge that they had rehabilitated themselves.

The bill reflects changing notions about adoption, she said. It should no longer be viewed as a vault that seals off a child's biological background, she said.

"Secrecy is pernicious. It's bad stuff," she said. "Adoptees think...

Meanwhile, Americans for Open Records does not believe Quackenbush's bill goes far enough, said Lori Carangelo, a Palm Desert woman who heads the organization.

"It would be better to leave all records open from the beginning, allowing courts to seal them only when good cause is shown, she said.

While Byrns waits for the federal case to get to trial and the laws to be changed, she wonders what became of Wayne Albert Bryan, born May 12, 1951.

She said her ex-husband put their son up for adoption while she was hospitalized with a broken back in 1952.

Children's Home Society of Cali-

'My mother must have been a hooker.' But once it's all out in open, and people know who people are, the fantasies go away."

Information also is vital to adopting parents who need to know about children's genetic heritage and the conditions in the families to which they were born, she said.

Some adoptive parents who were not told of the extensive psychological or physical injuries of the children before adoption have filed lawsuits against the states that placed the children in their homes, she said.

The primary argument against open records is that adopted children will turn up on the doorsteps of their birth mothers 18 years later, threatening by their presence to reveal the women's secret, she said.

fornia has told Byrns that her son was placed through its adoption agency in 1954, and his first name was changed to Jimmy.

In a letter to Byrns, the society said child-welfare authorities in San Diego County removed Wayne, his brother and two sisters from the custody of Byrns and her husband because of neglect.

Byrns denies she ever neglected her children. She has since found three of them, but not Wayne, the youngest.

Byrns has filed the necessary waiver of confidentiality. Her son has not, and Byrns is convinced that he does not know he was adopted.

"I just feel it," she said.

Orange County Register, Orange County, California – 4/29/90

Chapter 2.
Government Protected Child Stealing
Under FEDERAL LAW

1990-1993- Carangelo v. Connecticut (also cited as
    Carangelo, Schafrick et al v. O'Neill, State of Connecticut et al
    in the United States District Court of Connecticut;
1990- Amended Class Action Complaint;
1990-1993- U.S. District Court Docket, Rulings;
1993-1994- Carangelo, Schafrick v. Weicker, State of Connecticut et al;
1993- Petition for Writ of Certiorari, United States Supreme Court;
1994- Images of the Actual 4-Page Memorandum by Eric C. Nelson;
2002- Adoption Books;
2008-2015- Facebook – Familiar and New Voices;
2009-2016- "Dear President Obama"

1990-1993 – "Carangelo et al v. Connecticut et al," U.S. District Court

"Carangelo v. Connecticut" was originally filed October 4, 1990 as a class action by "*adoption affected persons similarly situated*," and filed directly in the United States District Court of Connecticut at New Haven, by permission Chief Judge Ellen Bree Burns, rather than in Connecticut's state court.

THE PLAINTIFFS:
- Lori Carangelo (birth mother- California/CT) aka AmFOR;
- Thomas William Schafrick (adoptee – Connecticut);
- Barry Jacobson (adoptee – Connecticut);
- Bernadette Bahner (Barry's wife, Connecticut);
- Christopher and Theresa (Barry and Bernadette's children);
- Christopher Lemoult (adoptive father – Connecticut);
- Carol Lemoult (adoptee, Chris' wife, Connecticut);
- Jessica, Heather, Jeremy, Shea, Katie Lemoult (adoptees – Connecticut);
- Richard LaVrado (birth father, Connecticut);

AMICAE CURIAE: ("Friends of the Court" from other states
    who filed briefs as being "similarly situated"):
- Jean Paton (adoptee – Colorado);
- Ron Frieborn (birth father – California);
- Sandra K. Musser (birth mother & activist – Florida);
- Eugene Austin (fathers' rights activist – Nebraska);
- Mary Louise Foess (adoptee – Michigan);
- Melanie Sandoval (adoptee –Washington DC);

THE DEFENDANTS:

- Connecticut Governor William O'Neill, for State of Connecticut;
- Probate Administrator Judge Glenn Knierim (represented by Attorney Henry Cohn);
- Judge David Lukens (represented by Attorney Henry Cohn);
- Judge Salvatore Diglio (represented by Attorney Henry Cohn);
- Amy B. Wheaton, DCYS Commissioner; and
- Jean Watson, CT Department of Children and Youth Service (DCYF); (Wheaton & Watson represented by Attorney Ann-Marie DeGraffenreidt);
- The Children's Center (represented by Attorneys Elizabeth P. Gilson, Kevin P. Walsh)

United States District Court of Connecticut, New Haven, Connectcut

Standing: Barry and Bernadette Bahner-Jacobson, Co-Plaintiffs
in the original 1990 Class Action Complaint,
with their children, Christopher, then age 7, and Theresa, age 8;
Seated: Tom Schafrick and Lori Carangelo, Co-Plaintiffs

Chief Judge Ellen Bree Burns,
United States District Court of Connecticut at New Haven

Left to Right: Attorney Henry Cohn; Probate Administrator Judge Glenn E. Knierim
(2012); Attorney Ann-Marie DeGraffenreidt
(for DCYF); Attorneys Kevin P. Walsh and Elizabeth P. Gilson
(for The Children's Center)

Federal jurisdiction was based on: (1) the important federal question raised by our Constitutional, and civil rights claims, and (2) the fact that a State Court is prejudiced in a suit against the State. Chief Judge Ellen Burns agreed.

The year before, Professor Stephen Wizner, of Yale University Law School Clinical Law Studies, intended for one of his law students to help us take up the matter, but that student moved out of state and the project was dropped in favor of Yale's prisoner cases.

Judge Ellen Bree Burns, who had been appointed by President Jimmy Carter, was 65 years old when she got our case. She retired at age 91 after almost 40 years on the bench. Judge Burns and I both graduated from Hamden High School, 20 years apart. While I had to drop out in my first year at Santa Barbara Community College in order to work full-time, she went on to Yale Law School as one of only 5 female students in the school. In the decade before "Carangelo v. Connecticut," Judge Burns had presided over mostly criminal cases – including those of Gambino and Genovese Mafia crime family members, and some of New Haven's notorious drug trafficking gang members, including one who murdered a witness and posed a threat to her life. But she was reportedly unafraid, and has been known to express empathy for victims. Called a *"trail blazer,"* a "wonderful role model," and "the nicest person you'd ever want to meet," *she seemed the ideal judge to hear our case.*

One of the first hurdles I had to overcome was the 3-year Statute of Limitations for filing our case, as it had been 21 years since the 1969 adoption of my son from which his and my claims arose, and more than 3 years since the adoptions that affected the other Plaintiffs. I based my argument about "timeliness" on the 1989 case by an adoptee, Cathy Yvonne Stone, who *"could not know* she had a claim" on the music rights of famed singer-song-writer, her previously unknown birth father, Hank Williams Jr. The Court agreed that the Statute of Limitations tolled (began) *"when she first knew"* Williams was her biological father and she won her inheritance. Similarly, my son and I *"could not know"* the extent of our claims until I first made contact with him on May 10, 1987, which fell within the "3 year time Statute of Limitations" for filing tort claims, as separate from our claims of civil rights violations.

Attorney Henry Cohn, *who represented the Judges*, got his JD law degree from University of Connecticut and was later also appointed Judge of the Superior Court of New Britain in 1997.

Ann-Marie DeGraffenreidt, *who represented the Connecticut Department of Children and Youth Services (DCYS),* earned her law degree from New York School of Law and Yale University. She was then Director of Program Development and Legal Advisor for the Education Division of DCF.

The attorneys representing The Children's Center were Kevin P. Walsh and Elizabeth Gilson. Walsh is still a Partner in the firm of Williams, Walsh and O'Connor, LLP, while Gilson has since been a solo practitioner. Ironically, Gilson, who opposed me in our civil rights case, won a Pro Bono Award in 2010 (as did Judge Knierim in 2012) and defended the human rights of 2 brothers from China who were detained at Guantanamo Bay for 8 years, challenging "a new *secret* detention policy," (as we had challenged Connecticut's adoption *secrecy* laws and policies), saying she did so *"because it was the right thing to do,"* even though she was vilified by the government, the press, and those in the legal field, as a *"traitorous terrorist lawyer."* Too bad she was on the wrong side in *our* case.

Judge Burns *granted* my Motion for a Court Appointed Attorney to represent us pro bono from court funds, after I submitted a list of over 200 attorneys I had previously solicited and who had declined to handle the case, most claiming *"conflict of interest."*

Burns appointed Attorney Robert E. Grant, of the Law Offices of George J. DuBorg in Wethersfield, Connecticut, to represent us. Grant got his JD law degree from American University in 1977 and was admitted to the U.S. District Court in 1981. A 2010 client review at MartindaleHubbell.com rated him as *"Honest, hardworking, very knowledgeable."* The State Bar listed his practice area and experience as: Residential Real Estate, Wills, Probate, Trusts and Estates, and Estate Planning – *not* civil rights claims. But he seemed to understand our issues and we could not afford a trial lawyer.

One of my claims stemmed from refusals by The Children's Center to open my son's adoption file "for the purpose of informing him or his adopter about my newly discovered, *inheritable* cardiac disorder and allergies to the drugs that treat it." "Best interests of the child," the vague concept used to justify removing children from their biological families and placing them with strangers, didn't matter once my son's adoption was finalized. Before I filed our suit, a journalist, Chris Janis, at *The New Haven Register*, did a front page story and sequels about my 18-year search for my son and efforts to have the agency or court communicate to my son, or his adoptive parents, my newly discovered, inheritable cardiac disorder and allergies to the drugs commonly used to treat it. Janis interviewed Judge Knierim asking him why he refused to do so. He replied that he **"had no authority to take such action."** The Children's Center had been saying the same thing. Yet when they became aware of the publicity about my search and the medical urgency, **they phoned my son's adoptive mother, Lois Schafrick, just to see if I had found him and made contact. The medical concern headlined in their local newspaper that could be life or death to my son, *was never communicated to his adopters.*** Once again, so much for "child's best interests."

One of our original Connecticut Plaintiffs who had identical claims was Barry and Bernadette Bahner-Jacobson. Their son and daughter, who then were ages 9 and 10, had an undiagnosed brain disorder. Doctors urged Barry to obtain his family medical history to determine a *genetic* illness. But because Barry is *adopted*, the adoption agency, as well as a judge, *refused* to open Barry's adoption file to even confidentially contact Barry's biological relatives, even without disclosing names. His mother's name remained sealed and no effort was made by the agency or Court to contact her.

The State Defendants – DCYS, Office of Governor, and the 3 Probate Court Judges – all claimed *"Eleventh Amendment Immunity" from suit* in their Motions To Dismiss. In my response, showing why they were *not* immune from this suit in this case, I argued that their immunity claim depended on whether they were being sued in "official capacity" or "personal capacity," Nevertheless, Judge Burns granted all of the State Defendants' Motions To Dismiss, based on their claims of "immunity."

That left only the one private Defendant, The Children's Center. On Christmas 1990, 3 months after amending our Complaint, our attorney, Robert Grant, notified me he was asking to be relieved as our counsel *"due to conflict of interest"* – the conflict being that he also represented the insurers of The Children's Center. Merry Christmas.

ORPHAN VOYAGE

CEDAREDGE, COLORADO 81413 • (303) 856-3937

July 14 1990

Ms Lisa Hamlin
ACLU Children's Rights Project
132 West 43 St.
New York N.Y.   10036

Dear Lisa

Perhaps related to Oscar Hamlin? Anyway:

I received from Lori Carangelo a copy of your letter to her, dated June 21.
I am not surprised that the ACLU did not offer her any assistance, as those
of us who have asked, over the years, have been always rejected. This has
always astonished me, as I used to think of the ACLU as a liberating force.
This, back in the days of the New Deal, when I worked for the NLRB.

At the outset of my work in trying to relieve the colonial status of adopted
qeople, I wrote to Roger Baldwin, and had a letter from him. He sounded interested, but I did not pursue it. I was new at this then. Today I would have.

When I talk to a black judge, and refer to this colonialism in adoption, he
has no trouble understanding me. He then acquires a reputation for opening
birth records on the request of the adopted person. Period.

But the ACLU has never recognized the true plight of the adopted person.

Your reference in your letter to "appropriate services and treatment" just
about sends me up the wall - despite my eightyone years- as it sounds so like
the professionals who have worked happily as colonizers.

As to referring people who need help with an attorney, why would you refer
to ALMA. They are people with large financial resources. Lori Carangelo is
not, and has worked very hard to get as far as she has. When the ACLU lost
its empathy for the enslaved, I do not know, but it certainly has.

Sincerely

Jean Paton

Enclosures: Manifesto: Baran and Pannor statement

Letter from Jean Paton to ACLU, referring to adoption as
"colonialism" – 7/14/90

41

AMERICAN CIVIL LIBERTIES UNION FOUNDATION

CHILDREN'S RIGHTS PROJECT

National Headqu...
132 West 43 Stre...
New York, NY 100...
(212) 944-9800
(212) 730-4652 FAX

Norman Dorsen
PRESIDENT

Ira Glasser
EXECUTIVE DIRECTOR

Eleanor Holmes Norton
CHAIR
NATIONAL ADVISORY COUNCIL

Marcia Robinson Lowry
DIRECTOR

Chris Hansen
ASSOCIATE DIRECTOR

Christopher Dunn
Jeffrey B. Gracer
Robin L. Dahlberg
STAFF COUNSEL

Lise Hamlin
PARALEGAL

August 24, 1990

Jean Paton
Orphan Voyage
Cedaredge, CO 81413

Dear Ms. Paton:

In response to your letter to us, the American Civil Liberties Union is an organization with limited resources and a long list of potential clients. We simply cannot take every case that comes our way. There are just not enough resources to meet the needs of everyone.

That said, when Ms. Carangelo wrote to the Children's Rights Project, she was writing to a group of lawyers who specialize in foster care litigation. I attempted to explain that in my letter Ms. Carangelo, a copy of which reached you, but it seems I failed to make that clear. We handle class action suits designed to reform government child welfare systems. We do not venture into adoption reform.

I wish you well in your work. And, no, I am not related to Oscar Hamlin.

Sincerely,

Lise Hamlin

cc: Lori Carangelo

[Note: What ACLU is saying here is that they would have a "conflict of interest" if they represented adoptees rights because they represent interests of foster care-adoption agencies.]

ACLU letter responding to Jean Paton
as to ACLUs conflict of interest – 8/24/90

I was devastated when Attorney Grant abandoned us, however justified, yet at the same time felt a rush of over-confidence from being in a federal court with a *woman* judge presiding, but also reminded myself of the saying, *"Anyone who is his own attorney has a fool for a client."* Still, there didn't seem to be much choice – either continue "pro per" or quit. I was not a quitter.

For four years, it appeared I was holding my own against The Children's Center's lawyers, as Judge Burns teleconferenced me into her court, to enable me to participate in the proceedings in New Haven without having to leave my Palm Desert, California home, while my son, then 20, who lived in Meriden, Connecticut, was present in the courtroom at each hearing, never questioned by Defendants, sometimes falling asleep.

During those 4 years, both sides were entitled to "Discovery" which I aggressively sought from The Children's Center. Tucked within reams of unimportant building maintenance reports that arrived at my mailbox from The Children's Center were the inflammatory "Memos" – memos that someone, whether accidentally or intentionally, had slipped into the pile. The in-house memos were written by The Center's staff **documenting claims of physical and sexual abuse to children in care of The Children's Center, without third party reporting or intervention.** It appeared that the accusations had been swept under the rug in the same manner that child sexual abuse cases were handled by the Catholic Church and in the successfully prosecuted Sandusky/Penn State matter. When the memos were in my hands, the abused children named in the memos were adults. I regret that, at the time, I did not search for them and directly ask them to come forward and testify in our case in order to show a *pattern of deceit and what is really hidden by "confidentiality" and "privacy" policies,* but I hoped Connecticut media to whom I sent the discovered Memos would want to investigate whether a cover-up had been going on throughout The Children's Center's 100-year history. They didn't.

By the time of the next scheduled hearing, when The Children's Center's attorneys took notice of my filing *with the Memos attached,* the Center's response was swift. It was in the form of a "Request for Protective Order" – a Restraining Order to Quash the child abuse information for "damage control." The Center's attorney claimed that I was violating the "privacy" of the "children" named in the memos by filing them with our publicly accessible pleading. My teleconferenced response not only addressed why a Restraining Order should *not* issue, but also how the matter was related to our case and that the public had a *"right to know,"* which outweighed a *"right of privacy"* that was never requested but imposed on those child victims *who were now adults.* Judge Burns decided in favor of The Center's argument that the "privacy" of the abused victims was more important than the public's right to know how The Center treats children. When Judge Burns asked me whether I had leaked the Memos about the alleged abuses to anyone, I replied honestly:

> *"Yes, Your Honor, I sent them to EVERY newspaper in Connecticut, and to some major newspapers and other media outside Connecticut."*

A loud "gasp" could be heard through my phone from 3,000 miles away, which my son later told me was the shocked reaction of The Children's Center's attorney, Elizabeth Gilson, who he said nearly fell out of her chair. Judge Burns then ordered me to recite the *names of the newspapers*. Having no attorney to advise me, I did not know that I was *not* compelled to disclose AmFOR's *mailing list*, just as journalists are not compelled to disclose *their sources*. In the United States, because of the broad protections granted by the First Amendment, a media outlet cannot be found in Contempt of Court for reporting about a case because a court cannot order the media in general "not to report on a case" or forbid it from reporting facts discovered, publicly and "freedom of the press" has extremely limited exceptions such as "*unless the media outlet is a party to the case*"and, in this case, I was both the publisher and the main party to the case. Another rare exception to "freedom of the press," was following the shootings of 5 police officers in Dallas, when police asked media NOT to film or report what was going on at the site of the shootings in order not to tip off the assailant who was not yet known and media respected that request. Of course, refusal to disclose or refusal to obey a court order risks a civil "Contempt of Court" charge, and even jail time. I considered opting to go to jail for the publicity, as Sandy Musser had done, but feared that an arrest record would haunt any of my future endeavors including employment. But also, despite that all of the newspapers received my information about The Children's Center's abuse coverup *before* Judge Burns granted the Protective Order, *none of them ran with the story.*

Motions that I was confident would be Granted, Judge Burns then Denied. It was necessary to appeal Judge Burns' denials to the Second Circuit Court of Appeals for that Connecticut District, which is in New York. That court decided that our claims of civil rights violations and its life-and-death repercussions were (I quote): *"frivolous."* However, the Denials enabled me to then Petition the Second Circuit Court of Appeals to hear our issues in the United States Supreme Court.

There is no "automatic appeal to the Supreme Court in any legal case. One can only ask the Appellate Court's *permission* file a Petition for "Certiorari" – a Writ asking the high court to review the decisions of the lower court.

On January 6, 1993, our case in the US. District Court, was Approved for filing *in the United States Supreme Court.*

In part because two of the sitting U.S. Supreme Justices at the time were *women*, perhaps mothers, I again had a false sense of security that we would ultimately prevail. But it's unlikely that the Justices had even viewed our case.

Our Amended Complaint in the U.S. District Court and our Writ for Certiorari in the US. Supreme Court follows.

LORI CARANGELO, a/k/a   FILING APPROVED 3-14-91
AMERICANS FOR OPEN RECORDS   Docket #66
(AmFOR), individually
and on behalf of all others   CIVIL NO. H-90-21 (EBB)
similarly situated,
vs.   OCTOBER 4, 1990
WILLIAM O'NEILL, GOVERNOR,
STATE OF CONNECTICUT, ET AL

AMENDED CLASS ACTION COMPLAINT

i. INTRODUCTION

Adoption is a statutory invention created to enable society to cope with children who are basicallyunwanetd, neglected, or born to parents unable to care for them. Additionally, it is potentially the end of the road solution, if all else fails, for abused, neglected, abandoned and at risk children who are in custody, care or supervision of the Defendant Commissioner of the Connecticut Department of Children and Youth Services ("DCYS"), or its predecessor agencies, to ensure for each of them an opportunity for a safe and healthy childhood and a sense of permanent "family."

Since adoption serves a vital societal interest, in the past, the legislatures' foremost concern among the various states in enacting adoption laws has been in the protection of the integrity of the adoption process. This concern necessarily included the protection of the individuals involved in that process. In effect, then, the legislatures have guaranteed confidentiality to protect both the integrity of the adoption process and the privacy of the people involved by sealing records.

Sealed adoption statutes prohibit anyone, including the adoptee, adoptive parents and birth parents, from obtaining access to adoptionrecords. Access is granted by legislative design only if the petitioner convinces the court that he has good cause for opening the records. However, courts have uniformly failed to articulate a standard for good cause, and are reluctant to open records. Therefore, under a sealed records statute, those who desire to obtain the information sustain a heavy, if not unbearable, burden of persuasion.

The statutes and laws governing adoption in Connecticut have changed but not really evolved toward one direction over the years as the dichotomy and increasingly apparent cross purposes of confidentiality and privacy versus integrity and constitutionality of the process of adoption clash. For example, until 1975, Connecticut gave the adult adoptees (that is, those who had been adopted as a minor and who have reached the age of majority) a statutory right to a copy of their original birth certificate (instead of the "new" bith certificate which substitutes the adoptive new names and the adoptive parents' names rather than identifying the birth parents). The legislature amended this provision with Conn. Gen. Stat. Scetion 7-53 to require that the adult adoptee obtain a written court order stating that the judge thought that the adoptee's obtaining the original birth certificate would not be detrimentaal to public interest or welfare of persons involved, i.e., adoptee, adoptive parents and birth parents. Again, a heavy, if not unbearable, burden of persuasion.

To ease this plight, but apparently only for adoptees who are or have been made aware of their adoption, some states including Connecticut have enacted legislation allegedly designed to guarantee a more reliable procedural route to obtaining "open records" provisions has shifted control of confidentiality and privacy from courts (which govern with a vague "good cause" requirement) to individuals or agencies for those affected by disclosure.

As of October 1st of 1987, Connecticut allows for a limited access of information through Public Act 87-555. This "new" statutory scheme permits a

1

voluntary registry system allegedlyreforming from an intermediary judicial system
previously in place.

Voluntary registry acts allow the adult adoptee and the birth or genetic
parents to register their consents to the release of identifying information.
Registry acts, however, do not give the adoptee or genetic parent the right to
records access. Rather, they merely require state governments or adoption agencies
to establish systems that facilitate the matching of mutual, voluntary consent
information release. Voluntary registration and consent offer protection to
involved individuals and the adoption process. The individuals and the adoption
process retain the protection of the confidentiality guarantee that exists under
sealed record laws, and the adoption process may theoretically be enhanced by
securing for the unsure birth parents a possibility of reunion with the adoptee.
Still, adoptees may find that registry acts provide inadequate solutions to the
problems of sealed records acts, because of the possibility the birth parents will
not register and no match will be made.

Under the present 1987 legislative scheme or further legislative compromise,
this Act (87-555) requires the Defendant DCYS and other agencies to maintain
registries for all adoptions.

Ignoring the fact that the current statutes are not self-operative, that is,
absent an inquiry by the adult adoptee, he or she will not be given this
information. Ignoring further, if they are not told they are adopted, they will not
know to look. This leaves the decision solely to the discretion of the adoptive
parents, DCYS and other agencies along with the eroding role of the probate court
as the sole safeguard to avoid "lifelong familial amnesia" and to facilitate
conveyance of necessary medical information.

Under the present and past systems in place by legislative compromises, the
state, by and through its agencies and adoption systems are to "speak for" or
protect all adoption interests.

Plaintiffs challenge certain unlawful policies and practices of the Defendant
officials of the State of Connecticut concerning the operation of Connecticut's
child welfare and adoption systems as it effects adoption-affected families.

Plaintiffs assert that Connecticut's child welfare and adoption system
endangers children it is charged to protect, causes harm to children it is charged
to help and has been allowed to deteriorate to the point of potentially causing
irreparable injury to all involved with "adoption affected" families.

Plaintiffs assert that the Defendants' actions and knowing inactions have
deprived the Plaintiffs, and all others similarly situated, of their rights as
guaranteed by the First, Ninth, Thirteenth and Fourteenth Amendments to the United
States Constitution; their rights under the federal Adoption Assistance and Child
Welfare Act of 1980 as amended, P.C. 96-272, 42 U.S.C. Sections 620-627, 670-679;
and their rights under Section 10 of the Article First of the Constitution of the
State of Connecticut, along with Article XXI amendments to Article Fifth of the
Connecticut Constitution.

Plaintiffs also seek redress and damages for certain acts and/or omissions
where permissable under the law.

II. JURISDICTION

1. This action alleging violationof Federal Statutes and the UNited States
Constitution is authorized by 42 U.S.C. Section 1983 and jurisdiction over this
action is confirmed by 28 U.S.C. Sections 1331 and 1343 (a) (3).

2. A declaratory judgement is authorized pursuant to 28 U.S.C. Sections 2201
and 2202 and by Rule 57 of the Federal Rules of Civil Procedure. Injunction Relief
is authorized by Rule 65 of the Federal Rules of Civil Procedure. An award of costs
and attorneys' fees is authorized by 42 U.S.C. Section 1988.

2

III. PARTIES

PLAINTIFFS

3. Plaintiff LORI CARANGELO, (aka Lorraine Marotti in 1969) is a bith or genetic mother whose child entered the adoption system that was in place in Connecticut in January of 1969. She is, and for approximately 20 years has been, a resident of the State of California, currently in the County of Riverside, City of Palm Desert. At the time of one or more of the causes of action herein mentioned, Plaintiff Carangelo was a resident of the State of Connecticut, County of New Haven, City of Hamden.

4. Plaintiff AmFOR (Americans For Open Records) is an unfunded adoption civil liberties organization networking internationally for adoption reform, and is comprised, at least in part, of members who are Connecticut residents and are either adoptees, birth parents or strongly interested as an adoption affected family member.

5. THOMAS WILLIAM SCHAFRICK, (allegedly aka Richard Marotti) is now an adult adoptee resident of the State of Connecticut. Allegedly, he may or may not be Plaintiff Lori Carangelo's genetic son.

DEFENDANTS

6. Defendant, WILLIAM O'NEILL, is, and at all times pertinent herein has been, Governor of the State of Connecticut or the successor for the previous Gpvernors. Defendant O'Neill is vested with the civil administration of the laws of the State of Connecticut and is empowered to take any action concerning the protection of the citizens of the state and is required to prepare a budget for the State. He is also authorized to apply for federal funds or to designate any commissioner, officer or agency of the state to apply for, accept, and expend federal funds allocated or payable to the state, to establish and administer or supervise the administration of any state-wide plan which might be required as a condition for receipt of federal funds, and to take all such other actions as are necessary to fulfill the federal requirements. He is sued in his official capacity.

7. Defendant, AMY B. WHEATON, Ph.D., is, and at all times pertinent herein has been, Commissioner of the Connecticut Department of Children and Youth Services. She was previously unidentified in the pro se complaint as a "DOE" Defendant for DCYS. As the chief executive officer of that agency, she is responsible for the overall operation, direction and supervision of DCYS, for initially preparing and finally administering DCYS' budget, for adopting and enforcing regulations and rules for the Department's operation, and for the administration of all state and federal funds received by DCYS for its programs and activities. She is sued in her official capacity.

8. Defendant, JEAN WATSON was at all pertinent times up to approximately June 1, 1987, the Social Services Coordinator for the Probate Administration for the State of Connecticut. Om or about June 1, 1987, and thereafter she accepted a "promotion" to DCYS and was the liaison officer to the public "regarding access to adoptionreords in Connecticut." Her title currently is "Manager of Adoption Services." She is sued in both her past and present official capacities.

9. Defendant Judge GLENN KNIERIM was, and at all times pertinent herein has been, up until the appointment of Judge David Lukens, Probate Court Administrator, in the Office of Probate Administration for the State of Connecticut, located at 186 Newington Road, West Hartford, Connecticut. He is sued in his official capacity.

10. Defendant Judge SALVATORE DIGLIO is, and at all times pertinent herein has been a Judge for the Hamden Probate Court. He is sued in his official capacity.

3

11. Defendant Judge DAVID LUKENS is, and at all times pertinent herein has been with the Office of Probate Administration for the State of Connecticut. He replaced Judge Glenn Knierim as Probate Court Administrator in 1989. He is sued in his official capacity.

12. Defendant The Children's Center and DOEs 1-5. The Children's Center, located in Hamden, Connecticut, is allegedly a private, non-profit, non-sectarian, multi-function social service agency. Founded in 1833, the Center was the first child-caring agency to be chartered in the State of Connecticut. The Outpatient Services Department provides counseling during and after pregnancy, short-term infant foster care, and adoption services. The department's Center for the Adoptive Community provides information, counseling and long-term support for adoptees, adoptive families and birth parents. The department also provides permanency planning for children in the care of the Department of Children and Youth Services. Mr. STREETER SEIDELL is or was the program director and Ms. SUSAN CABRANES-SACCIO is the Director of Outpatient Services (Adoption). The remaining "DOES" are unknown persons working at or on behalf of The Children's Center for the period of approximately January 1969 to the present.

IV. CLASS ACTION ALLEGATIONS

13. The named parties bring this action as a class action pursuant to Rule 23 (b) (1) and (2) of the Federal Rules of Civil Procedure.

14. Plaintiffs file this complaint on behalf of themselves and all other similarly situated "adoption affected persons," seeking injunctive and declaratory relief from the unconstitutional and unlawful actions and inactions of Defendants, as herein set forth.

15. The class Plaintiffs seek to represent of "adoption-affected persons" is composed of: 1) all children who were, are, or will be unwanted, neglected or born to parents unable to care for them and as a consequence of this "status" have or will enter into final adoption in the State of Connecticut; and 2) all children who were, are or will be in the care, custody or supervision of the Defendant Wheaton as result of being abused, negected or abandoned or of being found at risk of such maltreatment and who are potential furture adoption candidates as a termination of genetic parental rights is eminent or at least possible; and 3) all children who are, or will be, abused, neglected or abandoned, or who are or will be at serious risk of such maltreatment, of which DCYS knows, or should know and who are potential furture adoption candidates as a termination of genetic parental rights in eminent or at least possible; and 4) all post-final adoption children who would or will benefit from an adoption reunion registry; and 5) all post-final adoption adult adoptees who would or will benefit rom an adoption reunion registry; and 6) all post-final adoption children who would or will benefit from a registry facilitating the receipt of medical information; and 8) all birth parents who would benefit by a registry facilitating the recipt of medical information by adoptive parents on behalf of children under the age of eighteen; and 10) all adoptive parents who would benefit from a registry facilitating the receipt of medical information for the adopted children under the age of eighteen; and 11) all pre-final adoption foster parents who would benefit from the registry by facilitating the receipt of medical information for the child under age eighteen who is not yet in final adoption, but whose genetic parents' rights have been extinguished; and 12) all pre-final adoption children who would benefit from the registry facilitating the receipt of medical information on themselves after their genetic parents' rights have been extinguished.

16. Joinder of all members is impractical as the class includes many thousands of individual "adoption-affected individuals" at any one time and class membership fluctuates continuously.

17. There are questions of law and fact common to the members of the class.

18. The claims of the representative parties are typical of those of the class in that the constitutional and statutory deprivations alleged by the named Plaintiffs and caused by Defendants are the same as those suffered by all other class members.

4

19. The representative parties will fairly and adequately protect the interests of the class. The named Plaintiffs have no interests antagonistic to those of the class.

20. The prosecution of separate actions by individual members of the class would create a risk of inconsistent or varying ajudications with respect to individual members of the class which would establish incompatible standards of conduct for Defendants.

21. Defendants have consistently acted and refused to act on grounds generally applicable to the class, thereby making appropriate final injunctive and declaratory relief with respect to the class as a whole.

V. STATEMENT OF FACTS

A. STATUTORY AND ADMINISTRATIVE FRAMEWORK

1. State

22. The Connecticut General Assembly has declared the public policy of the State of Connecticut in regards to children to be: To protect children whose health and welfare may be adversely affected through injury and neglect; to strengthen the family and to make the home safe for children by enhancing the parental capacity for good child care; to provide a temporary or permanent nurturing and safe environment for children when necessary; and for these purposes to require the reporting of suspected child abuse, investigation of such reports by a social agency, and provision of services, where needed to such child and family. Conn. Gen. Stat. 17-38a(a) (February, 1965, P.A. 580).

23. Prior to this declaration, however, Connecticut had in place a statutory scheme concerning adoption. Until 1973 and Public Act 73-157, CGS 17-43a read as follows: "In any case in which the welfare commissioner determines that it would be in the best interest of any child committed to him that the child be given in adoption, the commissioner shall, prior to entering into an adoption agreement, petition the juvenile court for the termination of parental rights with reference to such child, including the right to petition the juvenile court for the revocation of the commitment of the child. The juvenile court <u>upon hearing after reasonable notice to the parents of such child</u> may grant such petition upon finding that over an extended period of time, <u>which shall not be less than one year</u>, except as hereafter provided, the child's parents (a) have abandoned the child in the sense that they have failed to maintain a reasonable degree of interest, concern or responsibility as to the child's welfare or (b) have failed to achieve any such degree of personal rehabilitation as would reasonably encourage the belief that at some future date they could assume a responsible position in their child's life or (c) have been or are unable by reason of continuing physical or mental condition to offer the care necessary for the well-being of the child and there are reasonable grounds to believe that such condition will be prolonged for an indeterminate period. When, in the discretion of the court, the interests of any foundling child will be promoted thereby, the court may waive the requirement that one year expire prior to termination by it of parental rights. When, subsequent to the commitment of the child as neglected or uncared for, the parent or parents of such child have executed consent to the adoption of the child, the commissioner may forthwith petition the juvenile court for termination of parental rights, <u>including the right of revocation</u>, an <u>upon hearing</u>, <u>following reasonable notice</u>, such petition may be granted if its ppears to be in the best interest of the child. Nothing herein contained shall negate the right of the welfare commissioner to petition subsequently the juvenile court for the revocation of a commitment of a child whose parental rights have been terminated in accordance with the provisions of this section; nor shall the granting of such petition affect the right of inheritance of such child, nor the religious affiliation of such child as it existed at the time of commitment." (1959, P.A. 184, S.1; Feb. 1965, P.A. 488) (Emphasis added).

24. Ub 1969, to fulfill the public policy, the Department of Children and Youth Services was established with P.A. 69-644.

5

49

25. P.A. 75-420 replaced welfare commissioner with commissioner of social services in C.G.S. 17-43a.

26. P.A. 76-226 replaced commissioner of social services with commission of children and youth services and for the first time, allowed an attorney representing the child to bring petition for termination of parental rights in C.G.S. 17-43a.

27. In 1975, P.A. 75-524 essentially rewrote the already codified Conn. Gen. Stat. Section 17-412, clarifying and extending the department's responsibilities to mandate the single budgeted agency "plan, create, develop, operate or arrange for, administer and evaluate a comprehensive and integrated state-wide program of services, including preventative services, for children and youth" who are mentally ill, emotionally disturbed, substance abusers, abused, neglected or uncared for, committed to it by any court, and voluntarily admitted to it for services of any kind.

28. DCYS is further mandated to provide: an effective program for the placement, care and treatment of children in its care; appropriate services to families and children and youth as needed; staff development and training; and aftercare and follow-up services appropriate to the needs of all children under DCYS care. It is also mandated to prepare biennially a five-year master plan which includes a written plan for the prevention of child abuse and neglect and a comprehensive mental health plan for children and adolescents. Conn. Gen. Stt. Section 17-412.

29. Further, the Connecticut General Assembly has imposed significant specific responsibilities on the Defendant Commissioner of DCYS. She, through her agents, is required to investigate all referrals regarding children who are reported to be abused, neglected, abandoned or at risk of such maltreatment, whether made by a professional mandated by state law to make such referrals, or by some other person, and whether made by written report or by phone, letter or other means. She, through her agents, is further required to conduct "immediate" inspections regarding all referrals to DCYS by state-mandated reporters of any child abuse, neglect or maltreatment, and "prompt" investigations of all other referrals, and, when a referral is substantiated, to take necessary action to protect the child who is at risk by being under the care of the same custodians. Her additional mandated responsibilities include that she: provide careful supervision of all children under DCYS' care and ensure that they have adequare medical, dental, psychiatric, psychological, social, religious and other services; maintain a variety of facilities and services for identification, evaluation treatment, and aftercare of children and youth in need of DCYS' services and administer them in a coordinated and integrated manner. Conn. Gen. Stat. Sections 17-32, 17-36 to 17-38c, 17-415, 17-446, 46b-129.

30. Chapter 310 of Title 17 of the Connecticut General Statutes is entirely devoted to DCYS exclusively and further codifies responsibilities and procedures.

31. In addition to all of the above, P.A. 87-55 entitled, "An Act Concerning the Availability and Confidentiality of Information Concerning Adoption and Termination of Parental Rights" literally heaped further responsibilities and duties upon the already overburdened and taxed Commissioner and DCYS.

32. P.A. 87-55 can be summarized as follows: This act makes a number of changes in the statutes regulating the access adopted people have to information about their background and their genetic parents and relatives. It retains the basic structure which requires general or "nonidentifying" background information to be accessible but which also places restrictions, including requiring consent, on access to information that allows an adopted person to identify his genetic parents and blood relations ("identifying information"). It expands: (1) those who may request information to include the children of deceased adoptees, and (2) those who may be inquired about to include adoptive as well as blood relatives. The act lessens the court's role in the process, allowing people who want information to go directly to the Department of Children and Youth Services (DCYS) or the appropriate adoption or child-care agency. The act abolishes the Adoption Records Review Board, which was created to hear appeals when people are unable to obtain information from

6

25. P.A. 75-420 replaced welfare commissioner with commissioner of social services in C.G.S. 17-43a.

26. P.A. 76-226 replaced commissioner of social services with commission of children and youth services and for the first time, allowed an attorney representing the child to bring petition for termination of parental rights in C.G.S. 17-43a.

27. In 1975, P.A. 75-524 essentially rewrote the already codified Conn. Gen. Stat. Section 17-412, clarifying and extending the department's responsibilities to mandate the single budgeted agency "plan, create, develop, operate or arrange for, administer and evaluate a comprehensive and integrated state-wide program of services, including preventative services, for children and youth" who are mentally ill, emotionally disturbed, substance abusers, abused, neglected or uncared for, committed to it by any court, and voluntarily admitted to it for services of any kind.

28. DCYS is further mandated to provide: an effective program for the placement, care and treatment of children in its care; appropriate services to families and children and youth as needed; staff development and training; and aftercare and follow-up services appropriate to the needs of all children under DCYS care. It is also mandated to prepare biennially a five-year master plan which includes a written plan for the prevention of child abuse and neglect and a comprehensive mental health plan for children and adolescents. Conn. Gen. Stt. Section 17-412.

29. Further, the Connecticut General Assembly has imposed significant specific responsibilities on the Defendant Commissioner of DCYS. She, through her agents, is required to investigate all referrals regarding children who are reported to be abused, neglected, abandoned or at risk of such maltreatment, whether made by a professional mandated by state law to make such referrals, or by some other person, and whether made by written report or by phone, letter or other means. She, through her agents, is further required to conduct "immediate" inspections regarding all referrals to DCYS by state-mandated reporters of any child abuse, neglect or maltreatment, and "prompt" investigations of all other referrals, and, when a referral is substantiated, to take necessary action to protect the child who is at risk by being under the care of the same custodians. Her additional mandated responsibilities include that she: provide careful supervision of all children under DCYS' care and ensure that they have adequare medical, dental, psychiatric, psychological, social, religious and other services; maintain a variety of facilities and services for identification, evaluation treatment, and aftercare of children and youth in need of DCYS' services and administer them in a coordinated and integrated manner. Conn. Gen. Stat. Sections 17-32, 17-36 to 17-38c, 17-415, 17-446, 46b-129.

30. Chapter 310 of Title 17 of the Connecticut General Statutes is entirely devoted to DCYS exclusively and further codifies responsibilities and procedures.

31. In addition to all of the above, P.A. 87-55 entitled, "An Act Concerning the Availability and Confidentiality of Information Concerning Adoption and Termination of Parental Rights" literally heaped further responsibilities and duties upon the already overburdened and taxed Commissioner and DCYS.

32. P.A. 87-55 can be summarized as follows: This act makes a number of changes in the statutes regulating the access adopted people have to information about their background and their genetic parents and relatives. It retains the basic structure which requires general or "nonidentifying" background information to be accessible but which also places restrictions, including requiring consent, on access to information that allows an adopted person to identify his genetic parents and blood relations ("identifying information"). It expands: (1) those who may request information to include the children of deceased adoptees, and (2) those who may be inquired about to include adoptive as well as blood relatives. The act lessens the court's role in the process, allowing people who want information to go directly to the Department of Children and Youth Services (DCYS) or the appropriate adoption or child-care agency. The act abolishes the Adoption Records Review Board, which was created to hear appeals when people are unable to obtain information from

6

51

the appropriate agency or court. Under the act, individuals may appeal to probate court when they are unable to obtain information or believe DCYS or an agency is not making a reasonable effort to obtain the information. Appeals from DCYS or an agency relating to nonidentifying information go to Superior Court. The act removes a requirement that an adult adopted person's adoptive parents be informed and consulted whenever the adoptee requests identifying information. It retains most of the consent requirements but alters some to make it easier in some cases for a person to obtain idnetifying information. The act requires agencies and DYCS to keep a registry of consents to the release of identifying information and to release such information whenever two parties to the same adoption have registered consents.

33. As early as 1977, P.A. 77-246 already created this registry for information for adult adoptees. CGS Section 45-686 as written in 1977 sets forth the legislative intent for the availability and confidentiality of records as follows: It is the intent of this part and Sections 7-53, 17-47a, 17-57a and subsebtion (c) of Section 17-431(1) to make available to adult adopted persons, adult persons whose genetic parents have had their rights terminated, adult persons whose genetic parents were removed as guardians and adult persons whose genetic parents' rights to custody were removed, information concerning their background and status and to give the same information to their adoptive parent or parents' (2) to provide for consensual release of additional information which may identify the genetic parents of such adult persons when release of such information is in the best interests of such persons; and (3) to protect the right to privacy of all parties to removal of custody, removal ofguardianship, termination of parental rights, statutory parent and child proceedings.

34. Also as of 1977, for those individuals (children) presently or at any prior time a ward or committed to the state, Subsection of Section 17-431(1) permitted and in fact often required disclosure by DCYS, or the previous state agency, of "communications and records" to individuals or public or private agencies engaged in medical, psychological or psychiatric diagnosis or treatment or education of the person.

35. If the gathering and limited release of non-identifying background and medical information of the genetic parents was not previously in the required records to be maintained on adopted individuals, it became necessary as made available after P.A. 87-555, Section 13 was approved and enacted. It reads as follows: "Sec. 13. (NEW) Notwithstanding the provisions of Section 45-68e to 45-68m of the general statutes, as amended by this act, the department and each agency which was party to, or participated in, either applications for approval of adoption agreements or termination of parental rights shall maintain registries. Such registries shall contain registrations of voluntary consents, refusals of consent and revocations of consent to the release of information which would identify the registrant. In the case where no agency was party to or involved in either proceeding, the Department of Children and Youth Services shall establish and maintain such registry. At any time following the termination of parental rights, the registration may be filed by: (1) a genetic parent who was a party to the proceeding for the termination of parental rights; (2) an-adult adopted person, an adult adoptable person, an adopted genetic sibling of an adoptable or adopted person, or an adult nonadopted geneti sibling of an adoptable or adopted person; (3) lineal ascendants and descendants of a deceased parent, or (4) an adoptive parent for the purpose of obtaining medical information which affects and adopted person. If a putative father is not a legal party to the proceeding for the termination of parental rights, the father shall present to the agency evidence of either the consent of the genetic mother or the death of such mother. No registrations shall be accepted unless the agency is satisfied as to the identity of the regsitrants."

36. CGS 17-431(e)(1) sets forth the unqualified right of access to DCYS records as it exists today, after P.A. 87-555, with no change from the original 1977 version: "(e)(1) In addition to the right of access provided in Section 1-19, the attorney of any person, regardless of age, shall have an unqualified right of access to any communications and records made, maintained or kept on file by the Department of Children and Youth Services, whether or not such records are required by any law or by any rule or regulation, when those records pertain to or contain information or materials concerning the person seeking access thereto, including but not limited

7

to records concerning investigations, reports, or medical, psychological or psychiatric examinations of the individual seeking access thereto; (2) any person or his authorized representative shall have the same right of access to communications and records set forth in subsection (e)(1) of this section, provided that if the commissioner determines that it wouldbe contrary to the best interests of the person or of the authorized representative to personally review the records, he may refuse access and advise that person or authorized representative of that person of the right to seek judicial relief; (3) when any person, attorney or authorized representative, having obtained access to any communication or record, believes there are factually inaccurate entries or materials contained therein, he shall have the unqualified right to add a statement to the record setting forth what he believes to be an accurate statement of those facts, and said statement shall become a permanent part of said record.

37. P.A. 87-555 repealed Section 45-68e. This new section now sets forth "Information available to adoptive parents and adult adopted or adoptable persons." It is requested that judicial notice be taken of this section rather than more fully setting it forth herein.

38. P.A. 87-555 repealed Section 45-68f and substituted a new Section 45-68f entitled, "Information regarding adoptions completed before October 1, 1977." Again, it is requested that judicial notice be taken of this scetion rather than more fully setting it forth herein.

39. P.A. 87-555 repealed the previous Section 45-68g and substituted a new Section 45-68g entitled "Agency or department to make efforts to obtain information." Again, it is requested that judicial notice be taken of this section rather than more fully setting it forth herein.

40. P.A. 87-555 repealed the previous Sections 45-68h, 45-68i, and 45-68j substituting new Sections 45-68h, 45-68i and 45-68j. Again, it is requested that judicial notice be taken of this section rather than more fully setting it forth herein.

2. Federal Statutory Framework

41. DCYS receives substantial federal funds pursuant to the federal Adoption Assistance and Child Welfare Act of 1980, codified as amended at 42 U.S.C. Sections 670-679 and 42 U.S.C. Sections 620-627.

42. The Adoption Assistance and Child Welfare Act of 1980 was enacted on June 17, 1980. The Act amended title IV of the Social Security Act (hereinafter "Act") and a new Part IV-E was created. This Act was designed to make needed improvements in child welfare and social services programs, to strengthen and improve the program of Federal Support for foster care of needy and dependent children...." (P.L. 96-272, Senate Report No. 96-336 dated June 13, 1980.) Title IV-E was developed in response to the growing number of children caught in what is commonly termed "foster care drfit." as well as to ..."prevent unnecessary removal of children from their homes and to....facilitate the return of children to their families."

43. Title IV-E provides Federal matching funds to the States to assist inoperating thestate's programs. State participation in this program is voluntary. If a State elects to participate in the Act, the State becomes eligible to apply for and receive federal matching funds. States are reimbursed for foster care and adoption programs as well as for some administrative costs depending on the number of children meeting eligibility requirements. However, in order to receive federal funds, the State must comply with all Federal laws and regulations and must submit a Plan which conforms with Federal requirements. (45 C.F.R. Part 1355 et seq. contains the federal regulations implementing this Act.)

44. Congress mandated that as each State adopts Title IV-E, the State would immediately implement its due process requirement of providing an opportunity for an administrative law "fair" hearing before the State agency to any individual whose claim for benefits available pursuant to this part (42 U.S.C. Section 670 et. seq.) is denied or is not acted upon with reasonable promptness. (42 U.S.C. Section

8

53

671(a)(12)). The fair hearing process pursuant to 42 U.S.C. Section 670 et. seq.
relating to child welfare services must be conducted in the same manner and be
consistent with the fair hearing process pursuant to 42 U.S.C. Section 602(a)(4).
The intent behind this administrative due process right of law is that those wishing
to be heard shall have an effective opportunity to be heard in an atmosphere that
is tailored to the capacities and circumstances of those who are to be heard. The
purpose of an administrative fair hearing is to offer an avenue of redress for
discretionary actions, inactions and arbitrary decisions. The procedure, as
outlined in 45 CFR Section 205.10 affords claimants certain and exact due process
rights that include timely and adequate notice, as well as what citeria shall
constitute a request for a hearing. 45 CFR Section 205.10(a)(11) specifies hearings
shall meetthe due process standard as set forth in this section.

 45. Congress further mandated that the State phase in two ther due process
requirements by 1983. These due process requirements are (1) each State must design
and develop a case review system for each child in foster care; and (2) provide
safeguards restricting the use or disclosure of information concerning individuals
assisted.

 46. In return for matching federal funds, the State must insure that each
agency and division within the State complies with the specific requirements
mandated by Congress.

 47. Each State, in its plan for child welfare services must designate a
single organizational unit, in the State or local agency providing child welfare
services, as being responsible for furnishing such services. (42 U.S.C. Section
622(b)(1)(B).) Such state agencies have the responsibility to ensure that all
requisites of the Act are adhered to by the counties and its contracted service
providers.

 48. This Act, and the Connecticut Plans submitted to and approved by the
Secretary of the United States Department of Health and Human Services in order for
DCYS to obtain funding pursuant to this Act, confer various rights upon children who
are in foster care or other out-of-home placements, or who are at risk of entering
such placements, or who are involved in situations with an acknowledged or perceived
end result of permanent adoption.

 49. DCYS receives federal funding pursuant to the federal Child Abuse
Prevention and Treatment and Adoption Reform Act, as codified at 42 U.S.C. Sections
5101-5106.

B THE NAMED PLAINTIFFS

 50. On or about February 14, 1968, a female baby was born to Lorraine Marotti
(nee carangelo) and Anthony Marotti in Santa Barbara California. Said child was
born in a breech selivery, two weeks early, and died within two hours of birth of
"congenital anomalies not compatible with life."

 51. Just prior to, or shortly after the death of this female baby, Lorraine
Marotti and her husband separated and he filed for divorce in New Haven,
Connecticut.

 52. Within a period of approximately one month after the delivery and death
of the female baby, a "separated" Lorraine Marotti became pregnant with a new
biological partner, a Jon C., not her husband.

 53. Some time prior to July 19, 1968, both parties (Lorraine and Anthony
Marotti) separately moved back to Connecticut as both were "local" and from
Connecticut originally.

 54. On July 19, 1968, a separated Lorraine Marotti starts a series of pre-
natal visits to Dr. George A. Bonner, M.D. in New Haven, Connecticut. As early as
the first visit, Lorraine Marotti recites the problems of her previous pregnancy
history and the resulting death of the female baby. In his office records, Dr.
Bonner notes the previous history taken, the fact that the patient is separated and

9

circles the word "welfare." Additionally, inhis examination notes, he writes of "systolic heart murmurs" without explanation, and estimates the pregnancy to be in the 14th to 16th week. He also takes the name of her obstetrician in California for the previous pregnancy and writes for those records.

55. On or about July 31, 1968, the divorce between Anthony and Lorraine Marotti became final in New Haven, Connecticut.

56. On or about August 12, 1968, Lorraine Marotti returns to Dr. Bonner reporting movement of the baby in the past week, the fact that she is now divorced and complaints of head cold and headaches. Lab blood tests are taken to "type" and "RH."

57. On or about September 5, 1968, Lorraine Marotti applies for, and receives benefits of Seventy-Six ($76.00) per month, from the City of Hamden Welfare, through her eighth month of pregnancy, receiving her last check on or about December 5, 1968 when she is switched over to the State welfare system.

58. Throughout the months of August to the delivery of the male child in December of 1968, an unwed, but pregnant Lorraine Marotti faithfully keeps her scheduled pre-natal appointments with Dr. Bonner where the fetal heartbeat is monitored, along with the mother's weight and blood pressure.

59. On or about December 17, 1968, at about 1:12 A.M. a male baby, "Richard Anthony Marotti" is born at St. Raphael's Hospital in New Haven, Connecticut.

60. The bill for St. Raphael and Dr. Bonner are assigned a welfare #067-NV-825912, effective 12-17-68 and apparently terminated January 7, 1969.

61. On or about December 20, 1968, Lorraine Marotti and a seemingly well infant baby boy were released from St. Raphael's Hospital.

62. Between December 20, 1968 up to and through January 7, 1969, both mother and child moved into the maternal grandparents' home and tried to cope with Mrs. Marotti's parents.

63. Within a few days of being released from St. Raphapel's Hospital, the male child developed what appeared to be digestive problems as he wouldn't eat or digest food properly and cried incessantly.

64. During the same period of time between December 20, 1968 and January 7, 1969, a blizzard struck and paralyzed the area, Lorraine Marotti was frequently hemmoraging and came down with the "hong Kong" flu.

65. Lorraine Marotti's efforts to care for her newborn child were often hindered by her own invalid mother's demand for rent payments and other monies while Lorraine hadn't enough money to feed the newborn or seek suitable housing for herself and child.

66. In addition to the flu and hemmoraging, Lorraine Marotti began feelings associated with "post-partum depression" after 18 months of continuous pregnancies.

67. On or about January 7, 1969, an "exhausted" Lorraine Marotti, her own father, Alfred B. Carangelo, and an apparently ill 3 week old newborn, sought help in the form of "temporary" foster care, upon the advice of a welfare social worker, to ease the obvious and overburdening economic, physical and mental pressures involved in their lives at that time, at The Children's Center, 1400 Whitney Avenue in Hamden, Connecticut.

68. It was Lorraine Marotti's belief and understanding with her father, as they eneterd The Children's Center that day, that once she had "recuperated" and was better able to provide for her again apparently ill son that she would again take over custody of the child. In the meanwhile, however, she would allow for a "temporary" foster care placement, and the medical care he needed..

10

69. It was neither the intent or desire of either Lorraine Marotti, or her father, Alfred B. Carangelo, as they enetered The Children's Center, to surrender the newborn male child for adoption and relinquish all parental rights.

70. On January 7, 1969, the newborn baby Marotti, aka allegedly now Thomas Schafrick, was not only suffering from digestive problems and incessant crying, but also was deaf from a painful undiagnosed developmental problem with his eardrums.

71. On or about January 7, 1969, The Children's Center, through a now unidentified employee or agent, represented to an apparently ill, exhausted and now distraught mother and crying newborn that they possessed no facilities or proceedures for foster care of children during a meeting between this now unidetified person, Lorraine Marotti and Alfred B. Carangelo in the presence of the newborn.

72. On or about January 7, 1969, The Children's Center, through the now unidentified employee or agent, refused foster care and indicated that The Children's Center would only accept the child and provide medical care and aid for the family's plight and that of the newborn child if the child was taken by the Center and relinquished for permanent adoption during this said meeting.

73. On or about January 7, 1979, The Children's Center had provisions and proceedures in effect for caring for children both for permanent adoption and foster care, as the agent or employee of The Chilren's Center then well knew.

74. On or about January 7, 1969, Lorraine Marotti and her father believed therepresentations of the now unidentified employee or agent of The Children's Center.

75. On or about January 7, 1969, during said meeting, based upon their belief of the false and fraudulent representationsconcerning the nonavailability of foster care, combined with physical and mental exhaustion, ongoing phsyical problems and in the presence of her incessantly crying newborn, Lorraine Marotti signed what was later learned to be a relinquishment of all praental rights to her newborn.

76. The false and fraudulent representations were willfully made on behalf of The Children's Center, by or through a now unidentified person with the intent of thereby deceiving Lorraine Marotti in order to induce Lorraine Marotti into siging a relinquishment and obtaining custody of the newborn for permanentadoption.

77. The relinquishment was obtained from Lorraine Marotti by the duress of the agent or emplyee in wrongfully deceiving, and further by the perceived threat acknowledged by the employee or agent to the health and well-being of mother and child, that immediate action was necessary not to further endanger life, in consequence of which, and in fear thereof, Lorraine Marotti executed same.

78. Neither Lorraine Marotti nor Alfred B. Carangelo ever received a copy of the relinquishment.

79. On January 7, 1969, the Marotti baby was placed in a foster home by The Children's Center.

80. For the period of January 7, 1969 to February 6, 1969, The Children's Center was paid for the "boarding" of the Marotti newborn infant a daily rate of $4.36 per day for a total of $126.44 by the Welfare Department of the City of Hamden, Connecticut.

81. Throughout the month of January 1969, Lorraine Marotti made numerous phone calls to The Children's Center inquiring about the baby and the baby's health and repeating her request for a copy of the "relinquishment."

82. After numerous attempts to contact Anthony Marotti, Lorraine's ex-husband, Mr. Marotti appeared at The Children's Center on January 31, 1969 to sign the papers as he was requested to do. He apparently was sent to the Hamden Probate Court to sign as the paperwork had been forwarded there already by a social worker

11

56

of The Children's Center.

83. In an attempt to regain custody of herchild, and to provide a source of finances away from the welfare system and her parents, Lorraine Marotti remarried within a month of January 7, 1969. This arrangement was entered into with a new husband, Fred C. Carbone, as he agreed to the same for the express purpose of regaining custody of the Marotti baby. Immediately, after a quick marriage, Fred C. changed his mind concerning his help and assistance.

84. On or about February 3, 1969, Lorraine Marotti made a formal request for the return of her child, but was informed that a "petition" had been sent to court.

85. Also on or about February 3, 1969, The Children's Center was informed that an attorney would be intervening on Lorraine Marotti's behalf concerning the child.

86. On or about February 3, 1969, The Children's Center was appointed guardian of the Marotti baby by the Hamden Court.

87. On or about February 3, 1969, the Marotti baby was placed in an adoptive home.

88. At some point in time after February 6, 1969, and which date is uncertain, the Marotti baby was formally adopted.

90. In the years of 1969 through 1974, Lorraine Marotti kept in contact with The Children's Center, despite her move back to California, and The Children's Center continued to refuse to provide any information concerning her child or a copy of the relinquishment papers.

91. On or about January 7, 1977, Eunice Baker, Adoption Supervisor for The Children's Center finally informed Lorraine Marotti, (now Lori Konzal) that the baby known as Richard Marotti was legally adopted by court action by his new family in the early part of 1970.

92. On or about August 4, 1977, then Governor Ella Grasso responded to correspondence from Lori Konzal (nee Marotti and Carangelo) and informed her of Public Act 77-246, which the Governor had signed into law on June 1, 1977. In said letter, the Governor wrote

"This Act allows for automatic disclosure of non-identifying information regarding the genetic parents of a child adopted prior to the law's enactment. This information, if available to the appropriate agency of the Department of Children and Youth Services, may be disclosed to adoptive parents as well as to adult adopted persons. I suggest, therefore, that you contact the Department of Children and Youth Services, 345 Main Street, Hartford 06115, for assistance in obtaining the data you desire."

93. On or about August 12, 1977, Lori Konzal wrote Mrs. Eunice Baker at The Children's Center and to the Department of Children and Youth Services following the Governor's advice. Additionally, in her letter to The Children's Center, Lori Kinzal inquired as to how she could determine whether her son's adoptive parents could communicate with her.

94. On or about August 18, 1977, Mrs. Eunice Baker wrote back indicating: 1) that the law did not go into effect until October of 1977; 2) that as much as possible non-identifying material regarding the child's background is given to the adoptive parents on the child's initial placement; 3) that the adult adoptive person after his eighteenth birthday can ask for identifying information provided the genetic parents are agreeable; 4) that she cannot be put in touch with the adoptive parents, but could pass on additional non-identifying information that Lori may want to put into a record if the adoptive parents ask for it; and 5) her prediction that nothing will be heard from Lori's son for at least 9 years.

12

95. On or about August 27, 1977, Lori Konzal wrote back to Mrs. Baker at The Children's Center expressing her disappointment that there were no provisions for the genetic and adoptive parents to communicate if they mutually desired and again requested a copy of "any paper I sugned when I surrendered my son, January 1969."

96. On or about August 31, 1977, Mrs. Baker wrote back indicating that she thought Connecticut has done a good job in giving protection to all parties involved in an adoption, and denying Lori's request for a copy of her child's original birth certificate and all documents or copies that were filed in court with respect to the adoption.

97. Again, on or about September 3, 1977, Lori Konzal requested directly to The Children's Center for "a copy of what I signed."

98. In September of 1977, Lori Konzal began writing letters to the editor of both local California and Connecticut newspapers seeking changes to the sealed adoption laws and periodically updated the "file" that The Children's Center was allegedly maintaining for her son if he at age 18 ever sought to look up and examine.

99. Also on or about September 6, 1977, Governor Ella Grasso responded further to Lori Konzal's correspondence indicating that the Governor had referred the matter to the Honorable Glenn E. Knierim, Probate Court Administrator for review of the suggestions for changes in the law and that the Governor was "sure that he (Judge Knierim) will be making recommendations in this area for consieration by the next session of the general assembly."

100. On or about September 16, 1977, Judge Knierim responded directly to Lori Konzal citing his belief that "If we are to keep a successful adoption process, it is our belief that such contacts should not be initiated by genetic parents and that after thorough study by his committee, he does not intend to present any new legislation in Connecticut along those lines."

101. On August 14, 1978, a Barry Baker of DCYS responded to Lori's 1977 letter written originally at the suggestion of the Governor, and stated then "Your letter to The Children's Center, where the childwas placed for adoption, has given them notice of your cooperation should the child or his adoptive parents request the information under PA 77-246."

102. On or about November 5, 1979, Lori Konzal wrote to the Children's Center for the name of its attorney as she would like to set up a Trust for the child.

103. On or about November 6, 1979, Lori was informed that Wiggins and Dana in New Haven were The Children's Center's attorney.

104. On or about February 1, and April 16 of 1980, Lori Konzal wrote to Wiggins and Dana regarding Connecticut trust, estate and adoption laws.

105. On or about May 22, 1980, an attorney, Clifford Grandjean, responded to the above inquiries and notes her request to have an ability to correct the birth certificate information. Attorney Grandjean states, "I enclos a copy of [SECTION] 7-53, which I read as extending to you the right to inspect the birth certificate, provided that a probate judge approves the inspection first."

106. In the year 1981, Lori Konzal was diagnosed with an inoperable cardiac problem and begins receiving Social Security Disability payments.

107. On or about April 11, 1981, Lori Konzal wrote to The Children's Center for a retrieval of the information she sent to "leave a trail" for her son.

108. On May 19, 1981, an "E.K.B." of The Children's Center noted that she had returned the registered material in the mail after making "copies of some of the returned things; this is a very mixed up person and is difficult to deal with" on a copy of the report.

13

109. On June 15, 1981, Lori Konzal wrote back thanking Mrs. Eunice K. Baker for her assistance and returns copies of all materials returned for placement in her son's file.

110. On or about April 19, 1983, The Children's Center acknowledged a receipt of Lori Konzal's letter of April 12, 1983 and indicates it will be inserted into her son's file.

111. On or about July 25, 1986, Lori Carangelo (formerly Konzal, formerly Marotti) wrote The Childre's Center to update her name and address.

112. On or about August 11, 1986, a Virginia Abbott of The Children's Center acknowledged the July 25, 1986 correspondence.

113. On or about December 12, 1986, Lori carangelo wrote to The Children's Center to Virginia Abbott with information concerning her child's "birth father" which had not been previously placed in The Children's Center's file for her son's access.

114. On or about December 14, 1986, the New HavenRegister ran an ad placed by Lori with a column and article concerning the ad with a headline which read: "Mom hopes ad will end adoptive mystery."

115. Later in december 1986, in a follow-ip story in the New Haven Register, the headline read: "Mother's Search for Son at Dead End."

116. On or about December 28, 1986, after her son's 18th birthday, Lori Carangelo wrote again to The Children's Center requesting information and again asking that the letter and attachments be placed in her son's file for his future access.

117. In the January session of the Connecticut General Assembly of 1987, a raised Committee Bill No. 1138 entitled "An Act Concerning Access to Medical Information" is introduced and referred to the Judiciary Committee. This act would provide for the transfer of medical information between birth and adoptive families (1) when it is needed for medical treatment in either family, (2) when it is needed for an adoptee's psychiatric treatment, or (3) when either party wants new information of a genetic condition given to another party.

118. On or about January 4, 1987, Lori Carangelo wrote to The Children's Center again requesting a copy of the relinquishment agreement and for a copy of her son's medical records while he was in the custody of The Children's Center prior to his adoption, including any record of his blood type if known.

119. On or about January 15, 1987, in a certified letter, Lori Carangelo wrote to The Children's Center requesting that she receive the following without a breech of confidentiality: 1) date of relinquishment; 2) copy of relinquishment agreement which she signed; 3) date adoption was petitioned; 4) date adoption was finalized; 5) ages of adoptive parents, profession and religion; 6) Court of jurisdiction regarding the adoption; 7) any medical information; 8) whether her son has contacted The Children's Center requesting information concerning his birthparents now that he is 18 years of age; and 9) copes of: (a) original certificate of birth, and (b) consent to adoption.

120. On or about January 16, 1987, Lori Carangelo wrote to Judge Glenn Knierim requesting: 1) verification of Court of Jurisdiction; 2) a request to file with Court "Waiver of Confidentiality" herewith; 3) assistance in obtaining information (dates) and documents:: (a) Dates of Relinquishment, Petition to Adopt, Finalization of Adoption; (b) non-identifying information about my son: Blood type, medical information; (c) Non-identifying information about adoptive parents (nationality/religion/jobs); (d) Documents I signed and was legally entitled to but have been denied, and paperwork generated up to adoption: (1) "termination of Rights" agreement; (2) "Relinquishment" agreement; (3) Original Birth Certificate and any medical records; (4) identifying information "for good cause."

14

121. On or about January 22, 1987, The Children's Center acknowledges receipt of the January 15, 1987 requests and informs Lori Carangelo that they are turning the matter over to their attorneys, Wiggin and Dana, requesting that all further correspondence be addressed through their legal counsel.

122. On or about January 27, 1987, a Jean Watson, Social Services Director for the State of Connecticut responded to the letter of January 16, 1987 addressed to Judge Knierim and indicated that they could not be of assistance without specifically addressing the requests contained in the January 16th letter.

123. On or about January 28, 1987, Lori Carangelo wrote to an Attorney Andrea Savoca of Wiggins and Dana requesting copies of all correspondence betwen The Children's Center and herself to date and a response to her certified letter requests addressed to The Children's Center.

124. On or about February 4, 1987, Lori Carangelo wrote to both the Probate Court in Hamden and the Probate Court in New Haven with her waiver of confidentiality consent and requests for documents, dates and non-identifying information which she was legally entitled to at the time of the relinquishment but never received along with a request that her adult adoptee son be contacted regarding her inheritable medical problems.

125. On or about February 5, 1987, Lori Carangelo wrote to Attorney Andrea Savoca to request to inspect her record of genetic information about herself as the "birth mother"; to provide information not already a part of the file concerning her "inheritable cardiac problems" which cause her to go into "complex arrhythmias" and the related allergies to some cardiac medications; and to provide communication as outlined in Section 45-68E of the Connecticut General Statute.

126. On or about February 7, 1987, Lori Carangelo wrote to Andrea Savoca to amend her previous requests to include a request that an outline of inherited medical problems and information regarding his genetic mother be provided to her adult adopted son citing Section 4 of the 1977 Act which pertains to a child adopted prior to 1977 that "information provided to an appropriate agency or Department of Youth Services may be disclosed to adoptive parents as well as adult adoptees."

127. On or about February 8, 1987, Lori Carangelo wrote to Andrea Savoca with documentation supporting her requests in the February 7, 1987 correspondence.

128. On or about February 19, 1987, Attorney Andrea Savoca representing The Children's Center wrote a 10-page cumulative response to the correspondence addressed to Wiggins and Dana refusing to convey any and all information concerning: 1) the date of relinquishment; 2) copy of Relinquishment Agreement; 3) copy of decree of termination of parental rights; 4) the date the adoption was finalized; 5) copy of consent to adoption; and 6) non-identifying information concerning the adoptive parents as this was now a part of the sealed court record of adoption and therefore The Children's Center through Wiggins and Dana were prohibited from providing the same.

129. In the same 10-page correspondence, The Children's Center claimed that all of Lori's pre-adoptive medical records, including Lori's son's blood type, were not a part of the sealed court records, but were a part of The Children's Center's sealed records and it was a policy of the Center not to release the same.

130. The February 19, 1987 10-page correspondence to Lori Carangelo from Andrea Savoca indicated that in unusual cases, the office of the Probate Court Administrator will unilaterally seek to provide important medical information to the adoptive parents. In relation to accomplishing this, Attorney Savoca advised that Lori Carangelo 1) prepare a statement for the file at The Children's Center containing the information and 2) have a medical expert prepare a report and letter to the Probate Court Administrator's office explaining the problems and requesting that the information be transmitted.

131. On or about February 25, 1987, Lori Carangelo sent a letter which included among other documents the support evidence outlined in Attorney Savoca's

15

letter regarding Lori's medical records and a physician's letter verifying Lori's genetically transmittable medical problems to the Probate Court Administrator Judge Glenn Knierim; the Probate Court in Hamden and The Children's Center along with several other addresses.

132. On or about March 2, 1987, a Joseph L. Paladino, M.D., wrote directly to Judge Knierim concerning Lori's permanent potentially genetically transmittable condition and the fact that such condition combined with her allergies could be life-threatening and his belief that this information should be passed along to the adoptive parents as well as Lori's son.

133. On or about March 5, 1987, Lori Carangelo wrote directly to Judge Knierim renewing her request for a communication to the adoptive parents of the existence of possibly transmittable medical conditions and enclosed a copy of Dr. Paladino's letter and requisite medical records.

134. On or about March 20, 1987, Jean Watson responded from the Probate Court Administrator's office that unfortunately, there was no provision in the statute for a birth parent to petition the Probate Court for transmittal of information, and therefore, the Probate Administrator's office could not assist Lori in this matter. She, however, requested The Children's Center to place such information in her son's closed adoption record.

135. On or about April 6, 1987, Attorney Savoca, acting on behalf of The Children's Center provided a copy of non-identifying information that would be made available to Lori's adopted adult son should he ever inquire with a provision to allow Lori to update said information.

136. On or about April 9, 1987, Lori Carangelo completes and/or corrects the forms sent from The Children's Center through Attorney Savoca and returns the same.

137. On or about April 9, 1987, Lori Carangelo renewed her request for copies of relinquishment agreement and consent to adoption to The Children's Center, through their attorney.

138. On or about April 22, 1987 the Probate Court Administrator's office, through Jean Watson, denied the request for a copy of the original certificate of birth to the birth parents once it had been amended as the child was adopted.

139. On or about April 22, 1987, The Children's Center, through their attorney, denied the renewed requests for a copy of the relinquishment agreement.

140. On or about April 24, 1987, The Children's Center, through their attorney, confirmed receipt of corrected non-identifying information on the forms provided and allegedly placed the information with their established file.

141. On or about April 28, 1987, Lori Carangelo renewed again her request for information and copies of documents relating to the relinquishment to The Children's Center through their attorney and a carbon copy to Judge Knierim.

142. On or about April 27, 1987, DCYS denied any involvement with this case and inferred that all information concerning closed adoption records must be directed to the agency involved in the adoption.

143. On or about May 19th (Mother's Day) of 1987, Lori Carangelo located who she believes to be her adult adopted son, a Thomas Schafrick through "underground" sources.

144. Thomas Schafrick's adopted parents separated in 1977, at which time he was told he was adopted.

145. On or about May 19, 1987, Lori Carangelo learned that Thomas Schafrick had an inherited condition causing deafness since birth requiring surgery and medical information from his genetic parents.

16

61

146. On or about May 19, 1987, Lori Carangelo learned that the adoptive parents of Thomas Schafrick were refused any and all information concerning his medical records going back to birth, after the adoption was finalized, despite their requests and the genetic mother's apparent consent to the release.

147. On or about June 16, 1987, Judge Knierim wrote to Lori Carangelo directly (not through Jean Watson) and indicated that the proper person, pursuant to Section 45-68i to petition the court for the original birth certificate is the adult adoptee and not the birth parents, despite the legal opinion of Attorney Grandjean in May of 1980. Judge Knierim further outlined the proper procedure and the final decision as being left to the judge of the particular court.

148. In summer of 1987, Thomas Schafrick petitioned the Probate Court for release of his original birth certificate which was granted and facilitated by Judge Salvatore Diglio of the Hamden Probate Court.

149. On or about August 21, 1987, Attorney Steven Wizner of the Jerome N. Frank Legal Services Organization of Yale Law School wrote the Judge he believed that transmission of confidential information could be implemented in the Probate Courts, pursuant to administrative direction, without passage of legislation. The confidential transmission would be the communication to adoptive children and their adoptive parents genetic health information provided by a biological parent after finalization of the adoption.

150. Senate Bill 1138 failed to pass in the 1987 legislature. The bill received a public hearing on March 28, 1987, but no further action was taken.

151. On or about September 18, 1987, Lori Carangelo wrote to Judge Knierim rebewing her plea for action by the Judge as suggested by Attorney Wizner in his August 21, 1987 letter.

152. On or about September 22, 1987, Judge Knierim responded to Attorney Wizner by enclosing a copy of Senate Bill 1138 and although ofering no explanation as to why the bill failed, attempts to engage Attorney Wizner to consider submitting a re-draft of said bill.

153. On or about September 22, 1987, Judge Knierim responded to Lori Carangelo's letter and indicated a willingness on his part to exchange ideas with Attorney Wizner, but requests that Lori direct all comments and questions to Attorney Wizner.

154. On October 1, 1987, P.A. 87-555 went into effect.

155. On or about October 7, 1987, Judge Knierim informed Attorney Wizner of a summary of a bill from DCYS to provide medical access which lists Gail Brooks as a contact. Said bill was to be a part of a packet of requested bills for 1988 that was submitted by DCYS.

156. On or about October 3, 1988, Lori Carangelo wrote to Judge Salvatore Diglio on behalf of herself and Thomas Schafrick petitioning the court to corect the original (pre-adoption) birth certificate as to paternity to reflect the true biological/genetic father in lieu of Anthony Marotti.

157. On or about October 21, 1988, Attorney Savoca returned to Lori carangelo copies on all correspondence written by Lori Carangelo and received by Wiggins and Dana on behalf of The Children's Center.

158. On or about October 26, 1988, Lori Carangelo renewed her request to Attorney Savoca that she return all correspondence between herself and The Children's Center (1969-1986) and not just that received directly by Wiggins and Dana on behalf of The Children's Center.

159. On or about December 5, 1988, Attorney Andrea Savoca reiterates that she sent all copies of letters received by Wiggins and Dana on behlaf of The Children's Center and refunds of $7.30 as that portion of ten dollars, as not being charged for

17

thepreviously copied and forwarded correspondence.

160.   On or about December 7, 1988, Lori Carangelo wrote to Judge Salvatore Diglio for action concerning her letter andrequests of October 3, 1988.

161.   On or about January 25, 1989, an Attorney H. Gordon Hall responded to Lori Carangelo's letter to the Attorney general concerning Judge Salvatore Diglio's failure to respond to herrequest concerning the proposed changes in the pre-adoption birth certificate of her son.   Attorney Hall wrote that although he believed that Judge Diglio would ultimately provide Lori with a response, she should direct further inquiry to the Probate Court Administrator who has an oversight on Probate Court activity.

162.   On or about February 28, 1989, Lori Carangelo wrote to Representative Richard Tulisano, Chairman of the House Judiciary concerning Judge Diglio's total inaction and urged him to re-introduce Senate Bill 1138.

163.   On or about May 3, 1989, Thomas Schafrick wrote to Judge Diglio requesting another copy of his pre-adoption birth cerificate and urged that the records be corrected to list his genetic father rather than Anthony Marotti.

164.   On or about May 17, 1989, Lori Carangelo wrote to Governor O'Neill requesting that he appoint a Governor's Commission to study Adoption Law in Connecticut.

165.   On or about June 26, 1989, Governor O'Neill responds to Lori carangelo's correspondence of May 17, 1989, indicating the 1987 change as significant with no further anticipated recommendations.

166.   On or about August 25, 1989, both Lori carangelo and Thomas Schafrick attempted to petition for ahearing with a pro se "Order to Show Cause" concerning respectively their October 3, 1988 and May 3, 1989 petitions.

167.   On or about August 26, 1989, a formal request for a fair hearing was made upon DCYS for "non-provision of service" by Lori carangelo and Thomas Schafrick in pro se.

.   168.   On or about September 1, 1989, DCYS through Barbara LDuc acknowledge receipt of the request for an administrative hearing.

169. On or about September 29, 1989, DCYS, following a review and assessment of the request for ahearing by DCYS and the Office of the State Attorney General, determined that no Statutory orRegulatory basis existed and therefore denied the hearing request.

170.   On or about October 1, 1989, both Lori Carangelo and Thomas Schafrick request that Judge Diglio be cited for Contempt of Court for non-response to the petitions of October 3, 1988 and May 3, 1989 and their pro se Order to Show Cause dated August 25, 1989 in a letter to Judge David Lukens as Probate Court Administrator.

171.   On or about October 3, 1989, both Lori Carangelo and Thomas Schrick compose and send a complaint concerning this denial of a fair hearing to Amy Wheaton, addressed as Director of DCYS.

C   THE CRISIS' IN CONNECTICUT'S CHILD WELFARE SYSTEM AND ITS SYSTEMWIDE VIOLATIONS OF THE LAW

172.   It is respectfully submitted that judicial notice gas been taken of a case entitled Juan F., et al v. William O'Neill, H-89-859 (AHN), that is currently pending in this United States District Court, District of Connecticut at Hartford.   In this case brought by Connecticut Civil Liberties Union Foundation and others as a class action by on and on behalf of all abused, neglected, abandoned and at risk children who are currently in the custodial care or supervision of DCYS, or those known or should be known to be subject to the

18

63

care, custody or supervision of DCYS by virtue of their similar status, the Plaintiffs challenged and alleged a myriad of unlawful policies and practices of the defendants concerning the operation of Connecticut's child welfare system as it affects their daily lives.

173. Alleged unlawful practices in said case includes:
- failure to investigate and protect children who are abused, neglected and at risof maltreatment.
- failure to ensure sufficient services to current out-of-home placements.
- failure to provide adequate care and treatment to children in DCYS' care.
- failure to ensure all children in DCYS' care receive necessary and appropriate treatment, and appropriate and least restriction placements by providing a complete continuation of care.
- failure to develop and implement plans to enable children to leave foster care and other out-of-home placements.
*- failure to move children to adoptive or other permanent homes when reunification is impossible.
*- failure to rpovide sifficient, trained staff to fulfill defenant's legal objectives.
*- failure to keep adequate records and information status.

174. These last three allegations (*), albeit all are troubling, are particularly important to the instant case and to the Plaintiffs herein. For instance:

1. On Adoption

a) Even when a child is available for adoption, DCYS fails to take appropriate and timely steps to obtain an adoptive home for him or her.

b) The number of DCYS children who are freed for adoptive placement far exceeds the number of licensed adoptive homes.

c) The gap between the number of DCYS children awaiting adoptive homes and the number of available placements has been markedly increasing. In June, 1988, there were 450 children awaiting placement and 146 licensed homes. One year later, in June, 1989, there were 541 DCYS children with parental rights terminated awaiting adoptive placements and only 166 licensed adoptive homes available.

d) Departmental studies of recruitment, licensing, and retention of adoptive homes have documented, and defendant Wheaton's own Budget Options have acknowledged, that additional services and support for potential adoptive families (such as increased pre- and post-licensing training, adoption supports and subsidies, and support services beyond the time of adoption), as well as additional staff to recruit, conduct home studies, and license, are necessary to increase the number of available, licensed adoptive homes.

e) Despite defendants' knowledge of the problem, defendants have failed to take the steps necessary to ensure that there is adequate recruitment, licensing, and training of sufficient numbers of appropriate adoptive parents to ensure that children in DCYS' custody will expeditiously be moved into adoptive homes.

2. On Failure to Provide Sufficient, Trained Staff to Fulfill Defendant's Legal Obligations.

a) Trained social work staff and supervisors, together with sufficient support staff, equipment and services are essential components of Connecticut's child welfare system.

b) Defendants have failed to maintain adequate numbers of DCYS caseworkers,

19

support staff, equipment and services to comply with DCYS' legal obligations under federal law.

c) Since SFY 81-2, the number of investigations of abuse, neglect, and at risk referrals completed by DCYS has nearly doubled. Since 1987, the average daily caseload served by the regional offices has increased by about 15%, and the number of abused, neglected or maltreated children who are in out-of-home care has increased by about 10%. The total numbert of currently authorized positions in DCYS, however, has failed to increase proportionately with this need for service.

d) Many authorized positions in the agency are vacant and defendants have ordered some of them to remain unfilled. Recent retirements underthe State's early retirement plan have exacerbated DCYS' staffing shortages. Only about 1/4 of the nearly seventy DCYS employees who recently retired, including more than ten social workers in the regional offices, currently are authorized to be replaced.

e) Staffing shortages are further exacerbated by staff who are unable to meet their job responsibilities because they are on workmen's compensation or leaves for medical or personal reasons.

f) As a result of defendants' chronic under-staffing of DCYS' social work force, the DCYS social worker staff have dangerously high caseloads that far exceed minimally-accepted professional standards and the professional standards as set forth in various state task force reports.

3. On Inadequate Records and Information Systems:

a) DCYS has no reliable system for identifying the individual children in care and tracking the actions taken for each of them on essential matters which are necessary to protect them, to ensure that they are to receive proper care, and to ensure a permanent placement. The computer system maintained by DCYS contains unreliable and inaccurate information which makes it impossible for DCYS to fulfill all of its various legal obligations.

b) In addition, DCYS' records on individual children and families are seldom complete, impairing DCYS' ability to fulfill its legal obligations to all children in its care.

c) In the Spring of 1986, a detailed study of DCYS' data processing services reported emphatically that DCYS' information system was inefficient. The SPY 87-8 Budget Option requesting additional funds to expand these services stated that "[y]ears of neglect in this area have seriously diminished the effectiveness and efficiency of the Division. The agency simply cannot reasonably respond to external requests for information and meet Federally mandated program reporting requirements. Most importantly, meeting the needs of its client [sic] base is becoming seriously impacted through the insufficiency of its automated support systems to provide timely and accurate information to the social workers in the field interacting with these clients."

d) Though aware that DCYS' records and information systems must be significantly upgraded to ensure that the needs of children in DCYS; care are adequately met, defendants have failed to remedy all the various deficiencies of the systems, thereby violating plaintiffs' right to receive services in a child welfare system with an adeqaute information system.

175. With all of the above, and apparently acknowledged problems with DCYS, it has been further acknowledged and admitted in a letter written to Plaintiff Lori Carangelo on or about September 13, 1989 from a Janice Gruendel, Deputy Commissioner of DCYS, that in the first two years the state registry existed, only 18 persons registered after 47 requested registration material for post-adoption reunions pursuant to P.A. 87-555 with only four "matches" resulting.

IV FIRST CAUSE OF ACTION - FEDERAL ADOPTION ASSISTANCE AND
                            CHILD WELFARE ACT OF 1980
    176. Paragraph 1 through 175 are incorporated herein by reference, the same

20

as though pleaded in full.

177. Defendants' actions and knowing inactions have deprived the plaintiffs and members of their class of the rights conferred upon them by the federal Adoption Assistance and Child Welfare Act of 1980, 42 U.S.C. Section 620-627, 670-679, including their rights to:

a)   periodic judicial or administrative review; and
b)   services in child welfare and adoption system with and adequate information system.
c)   appropriate and timely exchnage of information and further services for adoptees and their adoptive parents to address each child's medical needs prior to and after the adoption is finalized to assure each child's safe and permanent placement.
d)   proper care and medical treatment.
e)   further participation in Federally fuinded programs and services of DCYS.
f)   adequate procedures,trained and qualified personnel, and facilities to deal effectively with adoption cases.

V.   SECOND CAUSE OF ACTION - FOURTEENTH AMENDMENT TO THE UNITED
                           STATES CONSTITUTION - RIGHT NOT TO
                           BE   DEPRIVED   OF   STATE   AND   FEDERALLY
                           CREATED LIBERTY AND PROPERTY RIGHTS
                           WITHOUT DUE PROCESS.

178. Paragraph 1 through 177 are incorporated herein by reference, the same as though pleaded in full.

179. Plaintiffs and the members of the class enjoy certain liberty and property rights which have been created by mandatory state and federal law governing their respective protection, care and treatment, including but not necessarily limited to, the maintenance of records and placement. Defendants' knowing actions and inactions in administering a child adoption system which constitutionally denies plaintiffs and members of their class various of their liberty and property rights, deny plaintiff class members their right to due process of law so guaranteed by the Fourteenth Amendment to the United States Constitution.

VI. THIRD CAUSE OF ACTION - FOURTEENTH AMENDMENT TO THE UNITED
                           STATES CONSTITUTION - RIGHT TO CARE
                           AND PLACEMENT THAT IS CONSISTENT WITH
                           COMPETENT PROFESSIONAL JUEDGEMENT.

180. Paragraphs 1 through 179 are incorporated herein by reference, the same as though pleaded in full.

181. Defendants' knowing acttions and inactions in failing to provide children in their custody and/or under their supervision with care consistent with competent professional judgement has caused plaintiffs and members of their class to be deprived of their rights under the Fourteenth Amendment to the United States Constitution.

VII> FOURTH CAUSE OF ACTION - FIRST, NINTH AND FOURTEETH AMENDMENT
                           TO THE UNITED STATES CONSTITUTION -
                           RIGHT TO FREEDOM OF ASSOCIATION AND
                           FAMILY INTEGRITY AND RIGHT OF PRIVACY

182. Paragraphs 1 through 181 areincorporated herein by reference, the same as though pleaded in full.

183. Defendants have denied plaintiffs andmembers of their class their rights to freedom of aassociation and to family integrity, as guaranteed to them by the First, Ninth and Fourteeth Amendments to the Constitution by their failures including but not limited to: provide services and procedures necessary for proper and safe placement, the keeping of adequate and beneficial records on pending or recent adoptions, and failure to facilitate a possible later reunion between adoptees and genetic parents.   These acts or omissions interfere with familyrelationships so as to infringe their fundamental right of privacy.

21

66

VIII. **FIFTH CAUSE OF ACTION** - FOURTEENTH AMENDMENT TO THE UNITED
STATES CONSTITUTION - EQUAL PROTECTION -
CREATION OF A SUSPECT CLASS.

184. Paragraphs 1 through 183 are incorporated by reference, the same as though pleaded in full.

185. Sealed records legislation further complicated by inaccurate records keeping and the defendants' failure or omission to establish and implement proper procedures and other services in relation to adoption creates a suspect class and thus violates the equal protection guarantee of the Fourteenth Amendment. Theresulting denial of records access classifies them by their status at birth or a subsequent time to adoption and then such classification is comparable to others deemed suspect or quasi-suspect.

IX. **SIXTH CAUSE OF ACTION** - FIRST AMENDMENT TO THE UNITED STATES
CONSTITUTION - PENUMBRAL RIGHT TO
RECEIVE INFORMATION

186. Paragraphs 1 through 185 are incorporated herein by reference, the same as though pleaded in full.

187. The Defendants' acts or omissions in regard to adoption records information and registry denies the plaintiff their right to receive information in violation of the First Amendment.

X. **SEVENTH CAUSE OF ACTION** - THIRTEENTH AMENDMENT TO THE UNITED
STATES CONSTITUTION

188. Paragraphs 1 through 187 are incorporated by reference the same as though pleaded in full.

189. The Defendants' acts or omissions inregard to adoption records information and registry imposes not only the statutory barriers of the legislative action but further imposes an absolute barrier that results in lifelong denial of their natural origins thus "abolishing" or "robbing" them of relations with their genetic parents and thus are faced to wear a "badge or incudent" of slavery.

XI. **EIGHTH CAUSE OF ACTION** - SECTION 10 ARTICLE FIRST OF THE
CONSTITUTION OF THE STATE OF
CONNECTICUT

190. Paragraph 1 through 189 are incorporated by reference, the same as though pleaded in full.

191. The Defendants' actions and knowing inactions have deprived the Plaintiffs and members of their class rights confined upon them by Section 10, Article First of the Constitution of the State of Connecticut.

XII. **NINTH CAUSE OF ACTION** - ARTICLE XXI AMENDMENTS TO ARTICLE
FIFTH OF THE CONSTITUTION OF THE
STATE OF CONNECTICUT

192. Paragraphs 1 through 191 are incorporated by reference, the same as though pleaded in full.

193. The Defendants' actions and knowing inactions have deprived the Plaintiffs and members of their class of their rights confined upon them by Article XXI Amendments to Article Fifth of the Constitution of the State of Connecticut.

XIII. **TENTH CAUSE OF ACTION** - (AS TO THE DEFENDANT,
THE CHILDREN'S CENTER)

194. Paragraphs 1 through 193 are incorporated by reference, the same as though pleaded in full.

195. The actions and fraudulent misrepresentations of the Defendant, The Children's Center, through its agent or employee on January 7, 1969 wrongfully caused the Plaintiff, Lori Carangelo, to sign an alleged relinquishment agreement and permanently deprived her of the minor child then known as Richard Marotti.

22

196. The failure of the Defendant, The Children's Center, to produce a copy of the alleged relinquishment agreement has prevented the Plaintiff Lori Carangelo to this day of attacking its validity.

XIV. ELEVENTH CAUSE OF ACTION - (AS TO THE DEFENDANT,
                                  THE CHILDREN'S CENTER)

197. Paragraphs 1 through 196 are incorporated by reference, the same as though pleaded in full.

198. The omissions and negligent conduct of the Defendant, The Children's Center, through its agent or employee on January 7, 1969 wrongfully caused the Plaintiff Lori Carangelo to sign an alleged relinquishment agreement and permananetly deprived her of the minor child then known as Richard Anthony Marotti.

199. The failure of the Defendant, The Children's Center, to produce a copy of the alleged relinquishment agreement has prevented the Plaintiff, Lori Carangelo, to this day of attacking its validity.

WHEREFORE, the Plaintiffs respectfully request this Court to:
1. Assume and retain jurisdiction over this action.
2. Certify this action as a class action.
3. Enter preliminary and permanent injunction relief necessary and appropriate to:
    a) remedy the defendants' violation of the Plaintiffs' rights and the federal Adoption Assistance and Child Welfare Act of 1980 as amended.
    b) remedy the defendants' violation of the Plaintiffs' rights under the United States Constitution.
    c) remedy the defendants' violation of the Plaintiffs' rights under the Constitution of the State of Connecticut.
4. Enter a declaratory judgement declaring the defendants' policies andpractices violate the Plaintiffs' rights under the federal Adoptin Assistance Act of 1980 as amended, under the United States Constitution and the Constitution of the State of Connecticut.
5. Award damages as to the defendant, The Children's Center.
6. Award to the Plaintiffs their costs and attorneys fees.
7. Grant such other relief as the Court deems just and proper.

                    LORI CARANGELO, ET AL
                    PLAINTIFFS
                    BY: ROBERT E. GRANT, ESQ.
                    PRO BONO COUNSEL
                    FOR THE PLAINTIFF
                    100 GREAT MEADOW ROAD-4th FL
                    WETHERSFIELD, CT 06109

23

United States Supreme Court, Washington, DC

(photo courtesy of Library of Congress)

The 9 Justices for the October 1993 session
when Carangelo v. Weicker reached the United States Supreme Court:

First Row: Sandra Day O'Conner, Harry Blackmun, William Rehnquist,
John Paul Stevens, Antonin Scalia;
Second Row: Clarence Thomas, Anthony Kennedy, David Souter,
Ruth Bader Ginsburg

1993-1994- "Carangelo, Schafrick v. Weicker, State of Connecticut"

On November 11, 1993, our Petition for Writ of Certiorari was accepted and filed in the United States Supreme Court as "Case Number 98-683." Unknown to me, Eric C. Nelson, a corporate lawyer serving as Law Clerk to Justice Clarence Thomas, read our Writ and wrote a 4-page Recommendation to *Deny* Certiorari. Nelson's Memo was *sealed* in Justice Blackmun's files. Like our former court appointed attorney, Robert E. Grant, Nelson had NO *experience* with civil rights claims, but he certainly would have *understood* our claims. Nelson got his BA from the University of Wisconsin in 1989 and his JD law degree from *Yale Law School* in 1992, and was still an active member of the Wisconsin State Bar, and Partner in the Milwaukee firm of Foley & Lardner, LLP. But his areas of practice had been Commercial Transactions and Business Counseling to manufacturers, utilities and energy sources. Justice Blackmun's files, which included papers from Blackmun's final 1993-1994 term, were released for public access 5 years after Blackmun's death in March 2004. And it was years later that I learned the *reason* we were Denied Certiorari when I found those papers which were *then accessible* on Internet
[at http://epstein.wustl.edu/research/blackmun/Memos/1992/Denied-pdf/93-909.pdf]

Nelson opined that anything related to adoption *belonged in the State courts,* disregarding the prior decision by Judge Ellen Bree Burns, U.S. District Court, where the case had been filed and argued for 4 years, that our matter met requirements for *federal jurisdiction.*

On Page 1 of Nelson's opinions (images follow), Nelson referred to me as an "*unwed mother,*" not "divorced mother," nor just "mother." The vilified "*unwed mother*" is still an inflammatory political "buzz word" synonymous with "*welfare mother.*" Substitute "*Unwed Law Clerk*" to describe Nelson, and therein lies discriminatory stigma.

Nelson also stated we had *not* overcome the Statute of Limitations, *ignoring* the case of Cathy Yvonne Stone, an adoptee for whom the Statute of Limitations took a detour. If Judge Burns did *not* agree that we overcame Statute of Limitations per such citations offered, why were we in her federal court for 4 years? If she *did* agree, why did Nelson "*overrule*" her?

Nelson concluded his opinions on page 4 with his *incorrect* assertion that we had not "identified a split" – meaning he believed we hadn't shown a "*conflict*" between the decisions by the highest state courts, or between the federal Courts of Appeals in similar cases.

On January 10, 1994, the Court's Clerk, William K. Suter (not to be confused with Justice David Souter), informed us we were *Denied* Certiorari.

1993-1994 Petition for Writ of Certiorari, 2nd Circuit & U.S. Supreme Court

Docketed 11/18/93

No. 93-6838
In the
SUPREME COURT OF THE UNITED STATES
OCTOBER TERM, 1993

LORI CARANGELO aka AMERICANS FOR OPEN RECORDS (AmFOR)
and THOMAS SCHAFRICK,
-Petitioners pro se,
-against-
THE STATE OF CONNECTICUT; LOWELL P. WEICKER, Governor of
Connecticut; JEAN WATSON and COMMISSIONER, STATE DEPARTMENT OF
CHILDREN AND YOUTH SERVICES (DCYS);GLENN KNIERIM,SALVATORE DIGLIO Connecticut
Probate Court Judges; DAVID LUKENS, Connecticut
Prbate Court Administrator; and THE CHILDREN'S CENTER,
-Respondents.

**PETITION FOR A WRIT OF CERTIORARI TO
THE UNITED STATES COURT OF APPEALS
FOR THE SECOND CIRCUIT**

Petitioners, LORI CARANGELO (aka AMERICANS FOR OPEN RECORDS/AmFOR) and THOMAS
SCHAFRICK, herein respectfully pray that a Writ of Certiorari issue to review the
Mandate of the United States Court of Appeals for the Second Circuit in this action
on September 2, 1993, as to Appeal of the United States District Court of
Connecticut's judgement and opinions as to "Constitutionality" of statutes that
permit government protected child stealing under color of state adoption secrecy
laws.

Eric C. Nelson, corporate law attorney, Law Clerk
to conservative Justice Clarence Thomas, 1993,
and who Denied Certiorari in "Carangelo, Schafrick v. Connecticut"

71

i. QUESTIONS PRESENTED:

1. Does imposition of statutory secrecy in adoptions violate federally protected civil rights under the following Amendments to the United States Constitution:
 First Amendment (freedom of association, to receive information, and of family integrity and privacy);
 Ninth Amendment (fundamental rights, right to nationality and origins);
 Thirteenth Amendment (badges and incidents of slavery);
 Fourteenth Amendment (equal protection, right to care, creation of a suspect class, Liberty, Due Process)?

2. a. Do the adoption secrecy statutes which authorize falsification of the pre-adoption birth certiifcate and withholding and sealing, from access by the parties named in the Relinquishment of Parental Rights, Petition and Final Decree of Adoption, prevent the parties therein from effectively attacking the validity of these documents in a court of law at any time, and also help facilitate coverup of illegal methods of procurement? (particularly in this case where no statutory period for Revocation of Consent to an adoption has existed, past or present)?

 b. Do the challenged statutes prevent the statute of limitations from tolling on tort claims (Fraud, Negligence) by adoption affected persons when secrecy of records prevents them from knowing when they have such claims, until access to such records, or until access to one another?

3. Are the non-uniform adoption secrecy and disclosure statutes in the 50 states arbitrary and capricious because they reverse 200 years of agency policy as to open or public records in the absence of significant intervening change in circumstances "in the public interest" and because the change in policy admittedly was politically motivated?

4. Does the Eleventh Amendment shield judges, lawyers and government in this action?

ii. PARTIES TO THE PROCEEDING

The parties to the proceeding in the Second Circuit are those in the caption (appellants in USCA #93-7238, Civil, arising from District Court of Connceticut #H-90-21-EBB), including the 7 government Respondents and the 1 private Respondent.

24

26

The decision of the District Court of Connecticut is unreported and although this case was dismissed without review on merits, that Court opined this is a significant federal question, jurisdiction is properly within the District Court of Connecticut, and (in error) that the challenged statutes are "Constitutional." A copy of the Final Judgement and of the many decisions of the District Court is in Appendix B.

The decision of the Court of Appeals for the Second Circuit is unreported. That court neither permitted filing of Appellants' brief (although it was stamped "received" timely) nor addressed merits nor errors of the District Court cited in the brief. The Court's Mandate dismissed Plaintiffs-Appellants' appeal as "so lacking in merit as to be frivolous within the meaning of 28 USC Section 1915(d)", yet merits were never addressed in this case, nor may the courts "peek at the merits" without permitting Plaintiffs an opportunity to argue the merits also. A copy of the Mandate is in Appendix A, and the Docket page indicating timely receipt of Appellants' Brief is also in Appendix A.

JURISDICTION

Jurisdiction is established by the following:

1. Date of Court of Appeals for the Second Circuit Mandate, September 2, 1993 (less than 90 days from this Petition);

2. Jurisdiction turns on the federal question of Constitutionality of Connecticut's adoption secrecystatutes and was, in error, decided by the District Court without review of the merits.

3. "The federal courts may assume jurisdiction over casesarising from family law matters when there is diversity."
   -Carol Ankenbrandt as Next Friend and Mother of L.R. and S.R.
   v. Jon A. Richards and Debra Kesler, No. 92-367 on certiorari
   granted Jan. 10, 1992, Ct. of App. 5th Cir;
   -Ankenbrandt v. Richards, 91-4030, 5/1/91; AFFIRMED, E.D.
   La. and slip opinion Fed. R. App. 34(a); 5th Cir. R. 34.2

Petitioners, CARANGELO (resideing in California) and SCHAFRICK (residing in Connecticut), have Diversity, and their case arises from a family law matter--the relinquishment and adoption of Schafrick. The District Court approved these Plaintiffs (3/14/91) at Motion #56 to add Thomas Schafrick). Venue was established in the District Court of Connecticut. Both Plaintiffs appealed.

The United States Supreme Court, since Public Law #100-352 (in 29 Case Western 830, Vol 102, PartI, page 662) on June 27, 1988, has eliminated the United States citizen's right to automatic appeal on merits, contradictory to the intent of the framers of the United States Constitution and contradictory to legislative intent of the aforementioned amendment to the Federal Elections/Campaign Act, 2USCS Sec 437H n4. Traditionally, courts denied certiorari in individual and class actions by adoption affected persons similarly denied Due Process (as in ALMA Society v. Mellon, 601 F.2d 1225, 2d Cir.1979, cert. denied) but also the courts have conflicted, as in Mills v. Atlantic City Dept. of Social Services, 372 A 2d 646, N.J., 1977: "The burden ofproof is upon the State to demonstrate that good cause is not present to open records to an adult adoptee.") This conflicts with In reRoger B., 41 Ill., DEC 386 85 Ill. App: "An adoptee does not have a fundamental right to examine his adoption records." The challenged statutes conflict with other statutes of the same state (See Statement of the Case). United States Supreme Court Justice John Paul Stevens opined in the closely related DeBoer case on July 26, 1993:

   "Neither Iowa law, Michigan law, nor federal law authorizes   u n r e l a t e d persons to retain custody of a child whose natural parents have not been found to be unfit, simply because they may be better able to provide for her future and her education."
           -AD #64:   Jessica DeBoer aka Baby Girl Clausen By Her
                      Best Friend Peter Darrow v. Robert and Jan
                      DeBoer et al;
       and   -AD #65:   Roberta and Jan DeBoer v. Daniel Schmidt

28

The United States District Court, District of Connecticut, had jurisdiction pursuant to 42 USC Section 1983 (deprivation of civil rights under color of statute) under the First, Ninth, Thirteenth and Fourteenth Amendments to the United States Constitution, and also pursuant to 42 USC Sections 1331, 1343, 28 USC Section 2201.

Petitioners, CARANGELO (a relinqishing birth mother) and SCHAFRICK (Carangelo's birth son, an adult adoptee), bring this ation pro se and in forma pauperis, filed 1/10/93, USDC-CT claiming (1) wrongful adoption resulting in forcible separation of mother and son without the mother being deemed "unfit" and no statutoru scheme to revoke "consent"; (2) resulting from fraudulent misrepresentations of a social worker; (3) arising from SCHAFRICK's 1969 relinquishment and adoption; (4) covered up by imposition of statutorily sealed adoption records; (4) overcoming Statute of Limitations; (6) appealing courterrors. The aforementioned points are detailed in this section.

On or about January 7, 1969, CARANGELO sought medical care through temporary foster placement of her infant son (now SCHAFRICK) from Respondent, THE CHILDREN's CENTER who alleged that no temporary foster care nor medical care was avilable "at taxpayer expense," unless CARANGELO would give THE CHILDREN'S CENTER ustody of her baby." CARANGELO was not permitted to have a copy of what she allegedly signed, nor to ever again see her son, despite that she demanded his return the same day, unaware of the fraud. CARANGELO maintained contact with THE CHILDREN'S CENTER nearly every year for 18 years. Although there were many amendments to Connecticut adoption statutes, including concerning diclosure, there was never any statutory scheme for Revocation of the alleged relinquishment and her many attempts to regain her son were unsuccessful, therefore. All records concerning her son's relinquishment, subsequent adoption and his original birth certificate were withheld from her possession and sealed in Hamden, Connecticut Probate Court according to statute. Although CARANGELO has never been declared "unfit," she and her son were forcibly separated for life.

During 1986, CARANGELO attempted to communicate new medical information about her inheritable cardiac disorder and allergies to prescription drugs that treat the condition to her son or his adopters through the courts and agency that held his new identity and whereabouts secret, but she was denied due to lack of statutory scheme for transmittal of post-adoption medical updates. Her lobby of legislators to amend the statute and newspaper coverage of her efforts, as well as the proposed legislative bill, failed in 1986 and 1987. On 1/10/90, CARANGELO filed her original Complaint in this action in U.S. District Court of Connecticut; SCHAFRICK was later approved as additional Plaintiff.

On or about April, 1987, a Milford, CT. nurse, JANE SERVADIO, sold to CARANGELO her son's adoptive name and whereabouts for $2100 cash sent c/o SERVADIO by Federal Express to an unnamed informant allegedly employed within the Social Security/Welfare system with access to foster care records. CARANGELO and her alleged son, SCHAFRICK, were reunited on Mother's Day, May, 1987. For the first time, SCHAFRICK was informed by CARANGELO that they may have tort claims for fraudulent misrepresentations by THE CHILDREN's CENTER, which CRANGELO learned about in February 1987. And for the first time, CARANGELO learned from SCHAFRICK that he had been born deaf from painful punctured eardrums, left untreated by THE CHILDREN'S CENTER and undisclosed to SCHAFRICK's adoptive parents at time of placement. Later in 1987, the Hamden Probate Court granted SCHAFRICK a one-time release of his pre-adoption birth certificate (only) in 1987; that record is still sealed for life against any further access by the parties named in it. CARANGELO and SCHAFRICK have been many times denied access to the sealed court file as well as THE CHILDREN'S CENTER's file concerning this adoption, even under formal Freedom of Information Act requests and Discovery Motions in the District Court.

29

77

On or about March, 1993, the owner of an adoption search business, SANDRA K. MUSSER, aka Musser Foundation, was federally indicted as an accessory to receiving confidential information from an (unprosecuted) informant who is an employee of Social Security Administration, in United States v. Sandra K. Musser, 1:93 CR-96, USDC, OH-Ne, (3/93). Now-incarcerated (Prisoner #5193, federal Corrections Institute, Marianna, Florida) because her attorney "forgot" to stay the arrest while on appeal (USCA# 93-4105), Musser is regarded by The OpenRecords Movement as a scapegoat for unprosecuted geopolitical mass child stealers. And 900,000 Social Security employees have access to SCHAFRICK's records which are still denied to SCHAFRICK and CARANGELO though reunited.

> "I don't believe God ever intended for records to be sealed,
> for us to be separated from our own flesh and blood."
> -Sandra Musser to Ft. Meyers News-Press, 3/28/93, pg. 1-C.

Seealso Points and Authorities, page vii of this Petition, for cites from every major world religion's book of laws and testaments; they all reject obliteration of the adoptee's biological bonds and heritage.

Adoption-specific FOIA ruling leaves to discretion what is intended:
> "Information concerning adoption proceedings and home of
> prospective adoptive parents with whom minor was placed by the county welfare
> department after real parties in interest in guardianship proceedings
> relinquished custody of minor **was not absolutely privileged under this
> section.**"
> -CA Freedom of Information Act, Sec. 6255L Civ C Sec 22,
> citing Terzanian v. Superior Court In and For Alameda
> County (1970) 88 Cal Rptr 806 10 CA 3d 286.

> "....even if information reports did contain trade secrets,
> balancing of interests doctrine required disclosure
> in the public interest."
> -Uribe v. Howie (1971), 96-Cal.Rptr. 493 19 CA 194.

Controlling cases as to Constitutionality of statutes include:
> "All laws which are repugnant to the Constitution are null and
> void."
> -Marbury v. Madison, 5 US (2 Cranch) 137, 174, 76 (1803)

> "Where rights secured by the constitution are involved, there
> can be no rule making legislation which would abrogate them."
> -Miranda c. Arizona, 384 US 436 p. 491.

> "An unconstitutional act is no law; it confers no rights;
> it imposes no duties; it affords no protection; it creates no
> office; it is inlegal contemplation as inoperative as though
> it had never been passed."
> -Norton v. Shelby County, 118 US 425 p. 442.

> "The general rule is that an unconstitutional statute, though
> having the form and name of law, is in reality no law, but is
> wholly void, and ineffective for any purpose; since its
> unconstitutionality dates from the time of its enactment, and
> not merely from the date of the decision branding it. No one
> is bound to obey an unconstitutional law and no courts are bound to enforce
> it."
> -16 Am Jur 2d, Sec 177, late 2d Sec 256.

Concerning Statute of Limitations, the controlling case cites:

> "The Statute of Limitations tolls from the date Plaintiff first knew she might
> have a claim."
> -Cathy Yvonne Stone v. Hank Williams Jr. et al,
> 85-CIV-71 US Ct App 2d Cir (Dec. 5, 1989)

30

In the controlling case, Stone, an adoptee, could not know she had a claim on her famous faher's music copyrights until her adoption birth records were accessed and her birth father's identity known to her. In this case, CARANGELO could not have known she had a fraud claim until after a letter dated February 19, 1987 from defendant, The Children's Center's Attorney Andrea Savoca responded to her inquiry. The new Haven Register newspaper quoting CARANGELO and Children's Center employee in December 1986 supports that CARANGELO did not know of the fraud for over 18 years. SCHAFRICK could not have known until he was located by CARANGELO in May 1987. Both dates, when the parties "first knew" fall within the 3 year time prior to filing this action as required by the Connecticut Statute of Limitations for tort claims, which does not apply to their claims that their civil rights were and are still being violated since their records are still sealed from their access despite that the parties reunited in 1987.

District Court errors which denied Petitioners their Due Process are:

(STATEMENT OF THE ISSUES)

AS TO THE MANDATE BY THE UNITED STATES COURT OF APPEALS FOR THE SECOND CIRCUIT:

1. WHETHER the Mandate disposing of this case, in the interest of reducing caseload, as "so lacking in merit as to be frivolous within the meaning of 26 USC Section 1915(d)" (concerning pro se/forma pauperis Plaintiffs, fees and costs) discriminates against the pro se forma pauperis Petitioners in this case, and

WHETHER, therefore, Petitioners are deprived of Due Process;

2. WHETHER the Mandate of the Second Circuit inthis case is proper as it determines this case is "without merit" without review of the merits and without permitting filing of Appellants' Brief (received timely and without clerical or procedural problems);

WHETER, therefore, Pettioners are deprived of their Due Process.

AS TO THE JUDGEMENT AND OPINIONS OF THE UNITED STATES DISTRICT COURT, DISTRICT OF CONNECTICUT:

1. WHETHER the District Court improperly ruled as to Constitutionality of the statutes without benefit of jury decision in any court, past or present, nor of United States Supreme Courtreview, and without reviewing merits (or if the court "peeked at the merits," yet denied Plaintiffs an opportunity to argue merits);

2. WHETHER the statutes are Constitutional under the First, Ninth, Thirteenth and Fourteenth Amendments to the United States Constitution;

3. WHETHER children are property;

4. WHETHER it is the burden of the District Court, Jury or United States Supreme Court to determine 2 and 3, above;

WHETHER, therefore, Plaintiffs are deprived of jury trial and their Due Process, from 1969 to filing this action 1/10/90 to today.

5. WHETHER the District Court twice improperly denied Plaintiffs' Request for Entry of Default Judgement against Defendant, The Children's Center; and whether Defendants, Governor, State and Judges also defaulted;

WHETHER the District Court improperly granted the State defendants Eleventh Amendment immunity and therefore the Private Defendant was also improperly dismissed on basis of State Defendant dismissals in error;

Controlling case concerning Eleventh Amendment immunity ws advanced to the District Court inPlaintiffs' 11/26/91 rebuttal to the State defendants' 11/21/91 letter to that court. It cites:
    "It is not the capacity in which the suit is brought, but the

31

79

capacity in which Defendant violates Plaintiffs' civil rights under color of
state law....State officials may be sued for violating civil rights under
color of state law in personal capacity."
  --Hafer v.Melo, 112 S Ct 358, 362, 60 USLW 4001, No. 90-681
  on certiorary (Nov. 5, 1991) 90 DAR, Daily Journal DAR 13658

Also:
      "The purpose of judicial immunity is to protect the integrity   of the
      judicial process--not to shield lawyers--when the alleged invasion did not
      incur during the performance of acts that are not an integral part of the
      judicial process."
      --Donovan v. Reinbold, 433 F2d 738 (9th Cir. 1970)

In USDC Docket #136, Exhibit 11"Records: Judges" Vol III,#134.p.87:
      "If we are to keep a successful adoption process, it is our
      belief that such contacts should not be initiated by genetic
      parents"..."I do not intend to present any new legislation
      in Connecticut along these lines....It is my firm belief that
      it would, in the long run, do more harm than good...though it may cause
      hardship for certain individuals."
      -Hon. Glenn E. Knierim, then-Probate Court Administrator
      (who was lobbying and making laws while deciding cases)

      WHETHER, therefore, Plaintiffs are deprived of Due Process;

6.   WHETHER the District Court improperly ruled as to when the Statute of
Limitations tolled regarding Plaintiffs' tort claims in Counts 10 (Fraud) and 11
(Negligence); and

      WHETHER, therefore, Plaintiffs were deprived of jury trial
and their Due Process;

7.   WHETHER, withregard to the 10/30/92 Hearing on Order To Show Cause Why
Preliminary Injunction Should Not issue, the Court improperly withheld from public
record and access any pleadings, improperly withheld fromPlaintiffs the Rulings and
Trascript, and also improperly restrained and sealed 18 documents by not balancing
in favor of public interest overthe state's interest the statutory confidentiality
of records where evidence of sexual and physical child abuse while incare of
Defendant, The Children's Center, impacts on other children;

      WHETHER, therefore, Plaintiffs are deprived of Due Process;

8.   WHETHER the District Court improperly denied Plaintiffs' request for
Reconsideration on New Evidence That the State Department Documents Admit to
Government Protected Child Stealing Under Color of State Adoption Secrecy Statutes;
and whether the District Court is prejudiced as to federal agency policy; and

      WHETHER, therefore, Plaintiffs are deprived of jury trial and Due Process;

9.   WHETHER the District Court did in other ways obstuct justice by (1) preventing
Discovery, (2) denying replacement of conflicted court appointed pro bono counsel,
(3) not reading Plaintiffs' briefs due to backlog of 500 cases, (4) causing
Plaintiffs' first appeal (N92-7556) to be dismissed sua sponte due to District Court
granting appeal prior to issuing Final Judgement and causing such appeal to be out
of time, (5) closing case prior to Final Judgement, (6) denying Plaintiffs a copy
of the 10/30/93 Rulings and Transcript of hearing without cost due to indigency, and
from which Plaintiffs appealed without benefit of seeing them.

      WHETHER, therefore, Plaintiffs are deprived of jury trial and Due Process.

             CONSTITUTIONAL, STATUTORY, AND REGULATORY PROVISIONS INVOLVED
             (Please refer to STATEMENT OF THE CASE for precedents and to
             Amended Complaint in Appendix E, to support the following):

32

80

The Constitutional provisions involved include:

FIRST AMENDMENT - Freedom of association, to receive information, and of family integrity;
NINTH AMENDMENT - Fundamental rights, right to nationality and original;
THIRTEENTH AMENDMENT - Badges and incidents of slavery;
FOURTEENTH AMENDMENT - Equal protection, right to care, creation of a suspect class, Liberty, Due Process;
Also, the Federal Adoption Assistance Act of 1980.
The challenged statutes include Connecticut Civil Code sections (adoption/disclosure from adoption records) as follows:
17-38a(a), Feb. 1965 PA 580; PA 73-157, CGS 17-43a (1973);
PA 184, S1 (1959); PA 69-644 (1969); PA 75-420; CGS 17-43a;
PA 76-226; CGS 17-43a, 46b-129; Chapter 10 of Title 17 of CGS;
PA 87-55; PA 246 (1977); CGS 45-686; 7-53, 17-47a, 17-57a,
17-431(1)(c); PA 87-555, 9 13, 45-68e to 45-68m; CGS 17-431(e)(1); PA 87-555(e)(1)
and Sec. 1-9; PA 87-555, 45-68F (adoptions before Oct, 1977); PA 87-555, 45-68g, -h,
-i, -j; 45a-754, -752(a),-(e), 45a-743, 45a-756(a)(e), 45a-754(a)(e), 45a-755
(Registries), 45a-744(a),-(e) ("important state interest expressed by legsilature.")

The above statutes conflict with statutes of the same state as follows:
Connecticut General Statutes (West's) Vol. 28, Sec 53a-155 concerning tampering or fabricating physical evidence, a Class D felony;
CGS (West's) Ch. 93, Registrar of Vital Statistics, Sec 7-46, concerning completion of records and false entries.

In <u>Moore v. City of East Cleveland</u>, 431, US 494 (1977), Justice Powell wrote the proncipal Opinion for himself and three other Justices, concluding that an Ordinance limiting occupancy of a dwelling unit to a complicated definition of "single family" which recognized only a few categories of related individuals vilated the Due Process Clause since it constituted **an unwarranted invasion of family life**. Is not the forcible separation of family members and total obliteration of the child's origins through falsified birth records and the complex conditions for adult adoptee reunifications with birth families in Connecticut and some other states also **"an unwarranted invasion of family life"** for the sake of providing the child a caretaker? How does the State derive the right to be keeper of family secrets under the challenged "confidentiality" laws?

REASONS FOR GRANTING THE WRIT

I. THIS CASE PRESENTS A SIGNIFICANT FEDERAL QUESTION AS TO CONSTITUTIONALITY OF STATE LAW PERMITTING GOVERNMENT PROTECTED CHILD STEALING UNDER COLOR OF ADOPTION SECRECY STATUTES.

Petitioners have provided this Petition timely. But also, the time is ripe for addressing adoption sealed records and child stealing issues; therelated current cases involve similar deprivation of civil rights under color of state adoption secrecy laws -- including Justice Stevens' 6/26/93 Opinion in <u>DeBoer</u>, and <u>Musser</u> appeal. Government is telling us that we, the People, aren't worth anything. Courts aretelling us that we, the People, may not have Due Process, or that years of litigation will preclude the adoption affeted citizen from affording Due Process. The lawyer who defended the birth parents in <u>DeBoer</u>, Attorney Marian Faupel, approached bankruptcy and received death threats. Plaintiffs and Plaintiffs' witnesses received death threats. Neither the District Court nor Plaintiffs were able to find unconflicted counsel; court appointed counsel was relieved for conflict. Neither government nor courts understand consequences of their arrogance not only to Petitioners but to all citizens, when victims are denied Due Process and criminals are protected by secrecy laws. America's founding fathers wanted to avoid reliance on people in government instead of reliance on the rule of law (equal protection).

"State police power <u>not</u> authorizing that forbidden by national law is paramount."
-People v. Wood, 1928, 264 P. 298, 88 CA 621.

33

81

The District Court, relying on people in government (Attorney General of the State of Connecticut and State Defendants inthis action) and on the Second Circuit's past decision in ALMA Society Inc. v. Mellon, 601 F .2d 1225 2d Cir 1979, certiorari denied, in this action ruled:

> "The court dismisses this cause of action because the statutes in question are not constitutionally invalid."
> -3/14/92 Rulings, #176, Vol. II, #169, page 24, last line of para. 1.

But the District Court did not rely on "the people" -- that is, the jury--in this or any other case--to determine the Constitutionality of Connecticut's adoption "confidentiality" laws.

> "Only juries (the people) can enforce or judge the law."
> -State of Georgia v. Brailsford et al, 2 Dall. 1.

II. THE UNCONSTITUTIONAL STATUTES CREATE A "SEPARATE BUT EQUAL" CLASS DEPRIVED OF DUE PROCESS

The ALMA Court ruled:
> "...even if the statutes created a quasi-suspect classification, they withstood constitutional scrutiny because
> they were substantially related to an important state
> interest of promoting the social policies underlying
> the state's adoption laws."

Archibald Cox, Special Prosecutor, Watergate trial, determined:
> "A right is not a right in America unless it extends to
> all Americans."

The Constitutional safeguard of substantive due process requires that all legislation be in furtherance of a "legitimate government objective." Since the late 1930's, the Uited States Supreme Court has generally limited judicial review on basis of "substantive due process" to determine whether the law is rationally related to a "legitimate goal." Only when the legislation restricts whatthe Court characterized as "fundamental rights" will the Court allow stricter scutiny. Also in the 1930's, states began to enact statutes with regard to confidentiality of adoption birth records, without benefit of the Supreme Court's or the People's review. This 42 USC Section 1983 action alleges violations of Plaintiffs' civil rights under the First, Ninth, Tenth, Thirteenth and Fourteenth Amendments to the United States Constitution, by Defendants, in conspiracy and under color of statutes. The subject statutes concern falsification and sealing of adoption birth records from access by the parties named in them, in the State of Connecticut.

> "A 42 USC Section 1983 suit cannot be waged against the private defendant except where Plaintiffs allege conspiracy."
> -Francis Sobel v. University of Maine,597 F.2,51,1st Cir 1979

The Ninth Amendment rights are those so basic and fundamental and so deeply rooted in our society to be truly "essential rights" and "which cannot find support elsewhere in the Constitution." -576 F 2d 165.

The Second Circuit in ALMA and in this action, and the District Court inthis action, failed to statewhat the "important state interest" is nor what the "underlying social policies" are, in the 1930's or today. Nor did either court have benefit of jury trial or Supreme Court review of the first Constitutional challenge to New York's adoption secrecy statutes by a class action of adoptees in ALMA. Instead, the ALMA court and District Court in this action treats Plaintiffs and all other adoptionaffected citizens as "separate but equal."

> "Separate but equal violates the Constitutional guarantee of equal protection."
> -Brown v. Board of Education, 347 US 493, 1954.

The District Court stated (4/14/92 Rulings) "certain intrusions on the privacy of

34

the individual may be justified in the public interest," yet failed to support how intrusions are justified in the public interest.

> "There is no justification for government intrusion upon the privacy of the individual."
> -Griswold v. Connecticut, 381 US 479 (1965); and also
> -Roe v. Wade, 410 US 113 (1973).

The courts similarly dismissed other cases by adoptees, without jury trial, including Yesterday's Children v. Kennedy, 569 F.2d, 1977, certiorari denied. The Hawaii Supreme Court ruled, May 6, 1993 the burden of proof is on the ocurt to prove state's interest.

> "But the definition of 'undue burden' has been unclear since Justice Sandra Day O'Connor first used the words in an abortion case nine years ago--and unclear it remains."

III. a. The Second Circuit Erred by Mandating That This Case So Lacks Merit As To be Frivolous Within the Meaning of 28 USC Section 1915(d)- Thus Discriminating Against Forma Pauperis Appellants Whose Brief Was Docketed Timely Yet Filing of it was Refused and Merits Never reviewed - And Conflicting with District Court Openion That This Case Presents a Significant federal Question and with Precedents of Its Own and Other Courts.

    b. The District Court Erred by Judging Constitutionality of the Statutes Without Review of the Merits and Without Benefit of Any Similar case Decided on Merits and Conflicting with Precedents of Other Courts.

Plaintiffs in this action sought jury trial in federal court. A federal judgeship is not given exclusive right to judge the law. Congressmen, Senators, Presidents and Judges have no authority to enforce nor question the law.

> "There are no adversarial parties and the Judge may not question Constitutionality of the State of Colorado's confidential intermediary (adoption) statute."
> -In re Karin Jeanne Tomlinson, CO, Sup. Ct., 92-SA-108, and
> -In re Robert Sean Wood, 92-SA-136, 6/92.

In addition to conflict of interest from judges or anyone being paid from tax monies, "jury lawlessness" has long been established:

> "Jury lawlessness is the greatest corrective of law in its actual administration."
> -U.S. v. Dougherty, Note 32 at 1130.

> "The jury has the right to determine both the law and the facts."
> -Samuel Chase, US Supreme Court Justice, 1796, signing the Declaration of Independence,

> "I know of no safe depository of the powers of society but the people themselves; and if we think them not enlightened enough to exercise their control with a wholesome discretion, the remedy is to inform their discretion."
> -Thomas Jefferson, author of the Declaration of Independence

Jury lawlessness means willingness to nullify bad law. A jury could conceivably nullify the statutes requiring falsification and sealing of birth records, retroactively--just as the records were sealed retroactively and against the wishes of the parties named in such previously "open" or public records -- without necessarily nullifying all past adoptions, unless the adoption system itself is declared "unConstitutional" by a jury under Levy v. Louisiana, 391 US 68, 393 US 618; Armstrong v. Manzo, 380 US 545 (Texas 85 Sup. Ct.) -- landmark cases concerning parental notification.

The District Court states that this case

"also broadly challenges the State of Connecticut's
adoption system."
-4/14/92Rulings, #176, Vol. III, #169, page 1, line 1.

IV. NATIONAL SECURITY AND INTERNATIONAL RELATIONS ARE IN JEOPARDY --NATIONS ARE PROSECUTING ADOPTION AGENTS FOR STEALING BABIES (METHOS OF PROCUREMENT LAUNDERED UNDER STATE ADOPTION SECRECY STATUTES): ADOPTION INDUSTRY'S PRO-SECRECY LOBBY THWARTS BOTH DEMOCRACY AND CAPITALISM

Neither the interests of Democracy nor the interests of Capitalism are served when half of all the families inthe UnitedStates have a family memner who has been secretly adopted and who is, by law, denied access to their own unfalsified record about his/her own birth and adoption. Our State Department is under attack for mass kidnapping of foreign children to sell via the U.S. adoptionindustry (per USDC #260, 1/21/93 Motion for Reconsideration and Attachments, Vol. V. #251,and also Appendix F-1 hereto). The UnitedStates Special Rapporteur, Rights of the Child/Sale For Adoption project, calls the United States "the largest market for sale of foreign children into adoption." Several nations are prosecuting U.S. adoption agents for stealing babies for U.S. adoption while Congressional extremists are currently attempting to further "federalize" adoption under "uniform" subsidy and official kidnap standards under the same adoption secrecy laws of receiving states. (Appendix F documents)

Overall, early markers for violent revolution are already evident in sharp rises in divorce, child abuse, drug abuse, endemic lethal disease, violent crime, serial killers and those in our penal and mental institutions who are, disproportionate to the general and adopted population, American adoptees (Sources cited in this case: USDC Index To Record On Appeal, court approved/filed Exhibits in USDC #148, Exhibit #7: "The Adoptee, Medical and Psychiatric Issues," pages 1289 through 1140, especially 1323--serial killers who are adoptees, 1324--adoptees who kill their adoptive parents, 1327-30--adoption syndrome).

All facts stated herein have been argued and points and authorities cited in the District Court which can be reviewed "on the Record" except for the more recent opinions and decisions in DeBoer and Musser. One other significant event worthy of inclusion here is Petitioner CARANGELO's involvement in the DiLorenzo and Gill cases:

In her capacity as civil liberties advocate (aka AMERICANS FOR OPEN RECORDS/AmFOR), Petitioner CARANGELO has helped reunite thousands of adoptees and birth relatives, without charge, since 1989. She recently located the birth mother of adult adoptee, Melody DiLorenzo, when agencies refused to open this suicidal adoptee's adoption file. The birth mother had also been looking for Melody. In another case, on 10/4/93, CARANGELO's Proposal to the Parole Board at Arizona State Prison at Florence, and reuniting of incarcerated adoptee H.K. Noah Gill (ADC# 76631) with his birth mother and birth sister during his parole hearing resulted in the first parole being granted on humanistic grounds of the prisoner's "bad adoption causing his anti-social behaviors," now rehabilitatable as result of reuniting with his caring birth family who had also searched for him for over 30 years but were thwarted by secrecy laws.

CONCLUSION

The State of Connecticut and named Respondents in this action, as well as the United States District Court of Connecticut and the United States Court of Appeals for the Second Circuit have denied Petitioners their Due Process and jury trial and violated their civil rights as enumerated in the original and amended complaints and subsequent pleadings in the federal courts. The subject adoption secrecy statutes are also unConstitutional. Children are not property. It is the burden of the United States Supreme Court to determine Constitutionality of the statutes in this action.

Petitioners seek decalaratory and injunctive relief, Their original and amended complaints sought money damages to $18,000,000 -- one million dollars for each of the 18 years that CARANGELO and SCHAFRICK had been forcibly separated despite the

36

mother was never deemed "unfit." Thousands of adoptions are being legalized daily
in the United States without benefit of a United States Supreme Court decision as
to the Constitutionality of obliterating the adoptee's origins and medical history
and of covering up illegal methods of procurement in the process.

Respectfully submitted:

LORI CARANGELO, Petitioner pro se   THOMAS SCHAFRICK, Petitioner pro se
PO Box 401   PO Box 1856
Palm Desert, CA 92261   Meriden, CT 06450
(619) 568-2360   (203) 634-4319

JOINT APPENDIX OF THE RECORD
(Accompanied by Motion to be Excused from Printing
Portions of the Appendix, and Petition for Writ of Certiorari)

CONTENTS OF THE APPENDICES

37

85

No. 93-6837 .... I. F. P

U.S.C.A. 4
BRUCE THOMAS v. U.S.

11/22/93 - Cert.
FEB 28 1994 D

	GRANT	REFUSE	RULE
Rehnquist, Ch. J.			
Blackmun, J.			
Stevens, J.			
O'Connor, J.			
Scalia, J.			
Kennedy, J.			
Souter, J.			
Thomas, J.			
Ginsburg, J.			

No. 93-6838 .... I. F. P

U.S.C.A. 2
LORI CARANGELO & THOMAS SCHAFRICK v.
   LOWELL P. WEICKER, JR., ET AL.
11/18/93 - Cert.
JAN 10 1994 D

	GRANT	REFUSE	RULE
Rehnquist, Ch. J.			
Blackmun, J.			
Stevens, J.			
O'Connor, J.			
Scalia, J.			
Kennedy, J.			
Souter, J.			
Thomas, J.			
Ginsburg, J.			

No. 93-6839 .... I. F. P

U.S.C.A. 6

JOSEPH ARGENCOURT v. U.S.

09/20/93 - Cert.
JAN 10 1994 D

	GRANT	REFUSE	RULE
Rehnquist, Ch. J.			
Blackmun, J.			
Stevens, J.			
O'Connor, J.			
Scalia, J.			
Kennedy, J.			
Souter, J.			
Thomas, J.			
Ginsburg, J.			

No. 93-6840 .... I. F. P

CA - Calif.,
2nd App. Dist.
JOHN COOKSTON v. REGENTS OF THE
   UNIV. OF CALIF., ET AL.
05/23/93 - Cert.
JAN 24 1994 D

	GRANT	REFUSE	RULE
Rehnquist, Ch. J.			
Blackmun, J.			
Stevens, J.			
O'Connor, J.			
Scalia, J.			
Kennedy, J.			
Souter, J.			
Thomas, J.			
Ginsburg, J.			

<u>PRELIMINARY MEMORANDUM</u>

January 7, 1994 Conference
List 6, Sheet 5 (Page 36)

No. 93-6838-CFX

Lori CARANGELO, ET AL.   Cert to CA2 (Cardamone, Winter,
(upset w/ Conn adoption   Jacobs) (order)
secrecy statutes)

v.

WEICKER, Governor, ET AL.   Federal/Civil   Timely
(waives)

    1. *Summary*: Pro se petrs argue in a slightly disjointed petn
that Conn statutes dealing w/ adoption records are unconstl and
allow child stealing, and that the cts below denied them DP. This
splitless petn appears to be legally meritless. I recommend
denial.

    2. *Facts and Decisions Below*: Petr Carangelo alleges that,
as a young, ill, unwed mother in 1969, she was wrongfully induced

87

to relinquish her parental rights to her infant son by employees of resp Children's Center, an adoption agency licensed by the state of Conn. After years of attempting to contact and regain custody of her son, she claims to have been reunited in 1987. Petr Schafrick is the man Carangelo believes to be her son. Carangelo apparently is active in trying to reunite adoptees w/ their birth parents.

In 1990, petrs filed a rambling §1983 complaint in the dct against the governor and the state of Conn, the commissioner of the Conn Dep't of Children and Youth Services, 2 probate judges, the Conn probate ct administrator, and the Children's Center. They alleged that a number of Conn adoption-related statutes, particularly those dealing w/ the sealing of adoption records, violated their rights under the 1A, the 9A, the 13A, the EP and DP Clauses of the 14A, several state constl provisions, and the Federal Adoption Assistance and Child Welfare Act. Petrs also alleged fraudulent misrepresentation and negligence claims against the Center. Petrs sought monetary, declaratory, and injunctive relief, and attempted to bring the suit as a class action, the others in the class being all other "adoption-affected persons." It appears that the gist of petrs' complaint was that the statutes make it too difficult for adoptees and birth parents to review adoption records or to track each other down and exchange information if they are inclined to do so.

In 2 thorough opinions, the dct (Burns [sdj], D. Conn.) dismissed petr's complaint and denied class certification. The ct concluded that several of the causes of action were barred by the 11A, that others had failed to state a claim, and that "[e]ach of [petrs'] constl challenges to the adoption statutes fails because the statutes are rationally related to the important state interests in promoting the adoption process." Important to the dct's reasoning was Alma Society Inc. v. Mellon, 601 F2d 1225 (CA2 1979), cert denied 444 US 995, in which CA2 rejected similar constl challenges made to NY's adoption statutes. The dct concluded that petrs' tort claims against the Center were barred by the statute of limitations.

CA2 summarily dismissed petrs' appeal "as so lacking in merit as to be frivolous w/in the meaning of 28 U. S. C. §1915(d)."

3. *Contentions*: <u>Petrs</u>: [somewhat fragmented] The rulings of CA2 and the dct were incorrect and denied us DP. We were wrongly denied a jury trial on our constl claims. We were separated for 18 years even though Carangelo was never deemed unfit. The adoption secrecy statutes lead to the forcible separation of family members and the obliteration of adoptees' origins through falsified birth and medical records. They are unconstl. These laws allow "unprosecuted geopolitical mass child stealers" to continue their evil ways. "Our State Dep't is under attack for mass kidnapping of foreign children to sell via the US adoption industry." American

adoptees tend to be involved disproportionately in divorce, child abuse, drug abuse, violent crime, and serial killings.

4. *Discussion:* Although they make some interesting comments, petrs identify no split. They are obviously displeased w/ the statutory framework as it currently exists, but that concern is more properly addressed to the state legislature. The dct's rulings appear to have been correct.

5. *Recommendation:* DENY.

Response Waived.

IFP status appears proper.

December 18, 1993   Eric Nelson   Opin. in Petn.

CT/ Luttig/Yale

X SHC 12/20/93

January 10, 1994

Ms. Lori Carangelo
P.O. Box 401
Palm Deset, CA 92261

Re: Lori Carangelo and Thomas Schafrick
v. Lowell P. Weicker, Jr., Governor of
Connecticut, et al.
No. 93-6838

Dear Ms. Carangelo:

The Court today entered the following order in the above
entitled case:

The petition for a writ of certiorari is denied.

Very truly yours,

William K. Suter

William K. Suter, Clerk

2002 – Resulting Adoption Books

Following the conclusion of our efforts to seek relief in the federal courts, I turned my attention back to writing. In 2002, Schenkman scholarly book publishers published *"CHOSEN CHILDREN – Billion Dollar Babies in America's Multi-Billion Dollar Foster Care, Adoption & Prison Systems,"* an indexed documentary, since updated, that follows the dollars, names the special interests who profit, and explains how family dismemberment and over-incarceration feeds America's symbiotic, multi-billion dollar foster care, adoption and prison systems. The book and its subsequent editions also details the negative outcomes of its victims.

At the same time, Schenkman published *"THE ULTIMATE SEARCH BOOK – Worldwide Edition,"* intended to provide free or affordable self-help to adoptees and birth parents wishing to know and to locate each other, thereby lessening the need for my direct assistance or the need to pay hundreds to thousands of dollars for searches via "confidential state court intermediaries," or private "searchers."

Heritage Quest and other genealogical publishers published subsequent editions of *"The Ultimate Search Book"* in which I update state laws and search tips such as DNA testing for familial matches.

Email and Amazon spurred my over-night evolution from USPS mailing newsletters per the only Bulk Rate Mail permit issued by the Palm Desert Post Office at the time, and providing search assistance via mailed correspondence, to mass *e-mailing* submissions to publishers and media, and the "instant gratification" of self publishing e-books via Amazon, Barnes and Noble, and Google Books,' totally free self-publishing platforms. It also helped "give voice" to an ever growing number of adoptees and parents, and wrongfully convicted people, who would otherwise remain closeted.

Clearfield Books for Genealogical Publishing Company published *"THE ULTIMATE SEARCH BOOK- 2015 U.S. Edition"* and also *"THE ADOPTION AND DONOR CONCEPTION FACTBOOK – The Only Comprehensive Source of U.S. & Global Data on the Invisible Families of Adoption, Foster Care & Donor Conception."* At the same time, as aka Access Press, I self-published *"CHOSEN CHILDEN 2016 – People as Commodities in America's Multi-Billion Dollar Failed Foster Care, Adoption & Prison Industry,"* as an e-book with the new sub-title in keeping with growing public sentiment, then as paperbacks when Amazon enabled it.

2009-2016 – Facebook – Familiar and New Voices

For decades, I had been paying $50/hour to my "Web Guy," Keith Carangelo, (a software engineer and distant cousin by the same last name who I never knew or met), to build, edit, and update AmFOR's website with the images and text I email to him in Massachusetts.

92

AmFOR's website grew to more than 60 web pages, listed by alphabetical links on the right panel of the home page, along with the only totally free *"Donor Offspring /Parent (and Sibling) Registry"* which produced many "matches."

Then along came Facebook. Partly as a way to promote my books, and partly as a way to "stay current," I created a Facebook page that still displays each of my books at Facebook.com/l.carangelo. Before long, I had added 25 more Facebook pages and counting – most on adoption and justice issues – and over 4,000 Facebook Friends sharing their adoption stories and family rights issues. It's always a pleasant surprise to find not only old friends and even relatives on Facebook, but also adoption activists with whom I had previously had the privilege of working by mail and phone before Internet and email, and be able to now see, message, post, or chat with them without a long distance phone bill.

Sandy Musser was among many "voices from the past" with whom I re-connected on Facebook, and with whom I again "joined forces" to support petitions, e-mail-letter writing campaigns for legislation, and ideas, at her corner of Facebook called *"Adoption Activists Thinking Outside the Box."* But despite our combined number of Facebook Friends and Followers of both older and younger generations of "arm-chair activists" that we attract, most adult adoptees suffered from inertia when it came to *actively* participating in events to draw media attention to their issues. At most, they will gladly click a mouse to "Like" a page or to sign a petition for "open records."

In 2018 it was imperative that "millennials" vote in the Presidential election, especially those who are adoption affected, if they wanted change. Among the "newer kids on the block" at Facebook was Bastard Nation (BN). I commend their "no compromise" approach to open records legislation. However, like the NCFA's troublemakers of the past, some Bastard Nation members delighted in ridiculing and discrediting others' reform efforts that are not solely focused on BN's agenda. Despite that Bastard Nation and AmFOR were the "same side" regarding opening birth records, politically separatist lines were drawn even in Cyberspace, between pro- and anti- adoption groups, paid and no-fee searchers, adopters and "birth" parents.

2009-2016 – "Dear President Obama"

In 2009, America's first Black President, Barack Obama's, birth certificate became a central issue for Donald Trump who challenged President Obama's eligibility to be President. President Obama seemed our best bet for advancing the cause of unsealing adoptees' birth certificates as a *civil rights* issue. Sandy Musser and I rallied our groups to launch e-mail letter-writing campaigns to acquaint President Obama with our issues. Musser called on supporters to sign her *"Petition for An Executive Order to Restore Original Birth Certificates to Adult Adoptees by Enacting the Adoptees Restoration Act,"* which quickly garnered tens of thousands of signatures. And I called upon supporters to also sign AmFOR's *"Petition for an Executive Order for Natural Family Preservation Act"* aimed at curbing Government Protected Child Stealing and Trafficking – a "harder sell" that divided some followers.

93

Americans For Open Records (AmFOR)

January 28, 2013
(updated version of letter sent 2-16-09)
PRESIDENT BARACK OBAMA
The White House
1600 Pennsylvania Avenue NW
Washington, DC 20500

Dear President Obama,

You've addressed Gay Rights. Now is the time to address the "last civil rights issue" - and restore the civil and human rights of HALF THE U.S. POPULATION WITH AN ADOPTION IN THE IMMEDIATE FAMILY (loricarangelo.com/statistics), stemming from accident of one's birth and from adoption, and the need for **CHANGE** so that we, too, can move **FORWARD**.

CHANGE includes alternative forms of child custody *"in child's best interests,"* that do not impose lifelong secrecy and falsified birth records upon adult adoptees for *life* as every state now requires by law, along with non-uniform laws in some states that permit disclosure 18 to 25 years AFTER an adoption if impossible conditions are met.

Consider that the first thing American Slavemasters did upon purchasing African slaves was to change their names! Adoption is a throwback to the concept of "owning" another human being "as property" — also referred to as "colonialism" which you well understand (as did Lincoln). Hopefully the time for **CHANGE** has finally arrived.

Whether an adoption affected person simply wishes to know his true origins, or wishes to be President of the United States, the adopted child and adult does not have entirely the same control over his own destiny as non-adopteds. The **federal** sanction, *funding* and promotion of "legal" adoption of even **illegally procured** American and foreign children, **under state adoption secrecy laws**, as condoned by the U.S. State Departent, has worsened America's image as **"the largest market for stolen children in the world"** (see US State Department's "Pfund Memo" at "US OKs Child Theft" - loricarangelo.com/childtheft.html). .. and which must finally be addressed **in terms of civil and human rights** as

94

including well known serial killers school shooters and mass murderers, as to WHY they killed — because WHY their adoptions ultimately pulled the trigger is just as important as the control of the automatic weapons with which some of them killed)

Adding to competing interests of the child, of the biological parents, of the adopters, and of the State, is our Federal Government's ongoing intervention (and therefore obligation) regarding child adoption. Federal intervention is exemplified not only by federal subsidizing, tax breaks and promotion since the Reagan administration's "White House Support of The Adoption Option," but also by the much-revised **1994 Uniform Adoption Act which critics dub the "Evil Act"**, pointing out that the Act prevents adoptees from gathering sufficient information about their biological parents by sealing adoption-related court records for 99 years, provides insufficient periods for revocation of relinquishment of parental rights (to the delight of unscrupulous baby brokers), and does not properly require notification of a non-spousal father.

The United Nations "Rights of the Child" Conference and Hague Court's Intercountry Adoption Conferences, (for which I served as data reporting source by permission of the Special Rapporteur), side-stepped this issue as a matter of "diplomacy." The United States Supreme Court has also turned its back on adoptees by denying Certiorari re their 1970s and 1990s class action claims. For nearly seven (7) decades, attorneys have been saying the high Court is "not ready" to hear our issues. We say the time for **CHANGE** is now.

For further information and documentation compiled over the past several decades, supporting the need for **CHANGE** in the way we treat our nation's children (and solutions), please see "**CHOSEN CHILDREN**: *Billion Dollar Babies in America's Failed Foster Care, Adoption & Prison Systems*" - loricarangelo.com/ChosenChildren for link to the book at Amazon.com for KINDLE and at Barnes & Noble for NOOK.

Respectfully,

Lori Carangelo

LORI CARANGELO - https://LoriCarangelo.com
founder, AMERICANS FOR OPEN RECORDS (AmFOR) -
loricarangelo.com/amfor

Chapter 3:
Government Protected Child Stealing
And HUMAN RIGHTS

1992 – AmFOR as Data Source to The United Nations "Rights of the Child"
    Project; AmFOR's "Sale of Children" Report
1992 – AmFOR and The Hague Court's Intercountry Adoption Treaty

Universal Declaration of Human Rights

The "Universal Declaration of Human Rights" is the most commonly accepted statement of "human rights." It is a statement of principle that was adopted by the United Nations General Assembly on December 10, 1948. The 30 Articles establish the civil and political, economic, social and cultural rights of *all* people, as follows:

1. All human beings are born free and equal in dignity and rights. They are endowed with reason and conscience and should act towards one another in a spirit of brotherhood.
2. Everyone is entitled to all the rights and freedoms set forth in this Declaration, without distinction of any kind, such as race, color, sex, language, religion, political or other opinion, national or social origin, property, birth or other status. Furthermore, no distinction shall be made on the basis of the political, jurisdictional or international status of the country or territory to which a person belongs, whether it be independent, trust, non-self-governing or under any other limitation of sovereignty.
3. Everyone has the right to life, liberty and security of person.
4. No one shall be held in slavery or servitude; slavery and the slave trade shall be prohibited in all their forms.
5. No one shall be subjected to torture or to cruel, inhuman or degrading treatment or punishment.
6. Everyone has the right to recognition everywhere *as a person* before the law.
7. All are equal before the law and are entitled without any discrimination to equal protection of the law. All are entitled to equal protection against any discrimination in violation of the Declaration and against any incitement to such discrimination.
8. Everyone has the right to an effective remedy by the competent national tribunals for acts violating the fundamental rights granted him by the constitution or by law.
9. No one shall be subjected to arbitrary arrest, detention or exile.
10. Everyone is entitled in full equality to a fair and public hearing by an independent and impartial tribunal, in the determination of his rights and obligations and of any criminal charge against him.
11. (1) Everyone charged with a penal offense has the right to be presumed innocent until proved guilty according to law in a public trial at which he has had all the guarantees necessary for his defense.
(2) No one shall be held guilty of any penal offense on account of any act or omission which did not constitute a penal offense, under national or international law, at the time it was committed. Nor shall a heavier penalty be imposed than the one that was applicable at the time the penal offense was committed.

12. No one shall be subjected to arbitrary interference with his privacy, family, home or correspondence, nor to attacks upon his honor and reputation. Everyone has the right to the protection of the law against such interference or attacks.

13. (1) Everyone has the right to freedom of movement and residence within the borders of each state. (2) Everyone has the right to leave any country, including his own, and to return to his country.

14. (1) Everyone has the right to seek and to enjoy in other countries asylum from persecution. (2). This right may not be invoked in the case of prosecutions genuinely arising from non-political crimes or from acts contrary to the purposes and principles of the United Nations.

15. (1) *Everyone has the right to a nationality. (2) No one shall be arbitrarily deprived of his nationality* nor denied the right to change his nationality.

16. (1) Men and women of full age, without any limitation due to race, nationality or religion, have the right to marry and to found a family. They are entitled to equal rights as to marriage, during marriage and at its dissolution. (2) Marriage shall be entered into only with the free and full consent of the intending spouses. (3) *The family is the natural and fundamental group unit of society and is entitled to protection by society and the State.*

17. (1) Everyone has the right to own property alone as well as in association with others. (2) No one shall be arbitrarily deprived of his property.

18. Everyone has the right to freedom of thought, conscience and religion; this right includes freedom to change his religion or belief, and freedom, either alone or in community with others and in public or private, to manifest his religion or belief in teaching, practice, worship and observance.

19. Everyone has the right to freedom of opinion and expression: this right includes freedom to hold opinions without interference and to seek, receive and impart information and ideas through any media and regardless of frontiers.

20. (1) Everyone has the right to freedom of peaceful assembly and association. (2) No one may be compelled to belong to an association.

21. (1) Everyone has the right to take part in the government of his country, directly or through freely chosen representatives. (2) Everyone has the right of equal access to public service in his country. (3) The will of the people shall be the basis of the authority of government; this shall be expressed in periodic and genuine elections which shall be by universal and equal suffrage and shall be held by secret vote or by equivalent free voting procedures.

22. Everyone, as a member of society, has the right to social security and is entitled to realization, through national effort and international cooperation and in accordance with the organization and resources of each State, of the economic, social and cultural rights indispensable for his dignity and the free development of his personality.

23. (1) Everyone has the right to work, to free choice of employment, to just and favorable conditions of work and to protection against unemployment. (2) Everyone, without any discrimination, has the right to equal pay for equal work. (3) Everyone who works has the right to just and favorable remuneration ensuring for himself and his family an existence worthy of human dignity, and supplemented, if necessary, by other means of social protection. (4) Everyone has the right to form and to join trade unions for the protection of his interests.

24. Everyone has the right to rest and leisure, including reasonable limitation of working hours and periodic holidays with pay.

25. (1) Everyone has the right to a standard of living adequate for the health and well-being of himself and of his family, including food, clothing, housing and medical care and necessary social services, and the right to security in the event of unemployment, sickness, disability, widowhood, old age or other lack of livelihood in circumstances beyond his control. (2) *Motherhood and childhood are entitled to special care and assistance. All children, <u>whether born in or out of wedlock,</u> shall enjoy the same social protection.*

26. (1) Everyone has the right to education. Education shall be free, at least in the elementary and fundamental stages. Elementary education shall be compulsory. Technical and professional education shall be made generally available and higher education shall be equally accessible to all on the basis of merit. (2) Education shall be directed to the full development of the human personality and to the strengthening of respect for human rights and fundamental freedoms. It shall promote understanding, tolerance and friendship among all nations, racial or religious groups, and shall further the activities of the United Nations for the maintenance of peace. (3) Parents have a prior right to choose the kind of education that shall be given to their children.

27. (1) Everyone has the right freely to participate in the cultural life of the community, to enjoy the arts and to share in scientific advancement and its benefits. (2) Everyone has the right to the protection of the moral and material interests resulting from any scientific, literary or artistic production of which he is the author.

28. Everyone is entitled to a social and international order in which the rights and freedoms set forth in this Declaration can be fully realized.

29. (1) Everyone has duties to the community in which alone the free and full development of his personality is possible. (2) In the exercise of his rights and freedoms, everyone shall be subject only to such limitations as are determined by law solely for the purpose of securing due recognition and respect for the rights and freedoms of others and of meeting the just requirements of morality, public order and the general welfare in a democratic society. (3) These rights and freedoms may in no case be exercised contrary to the purposes and principles of the United Nations.

30. Nothing in this Declaration may be interpreted as implying for any State, group or person any right to engage in any activity or to perform any act aimed at the destruction of any of the rights and freedoms set forth herein.

Vitit Muntharborn, Special Rapporteur
to the United Nations Economic and Social Council
Commission on Human Rights
in Accordance with Commission Resolution 1990/68
"Rights of the Child"

1992 – AmFOR, Data Source to the United Nations "Rights of the Child" Project

The United Nations' "Rights of the Child" Project identified the United States as *"the largest market for stolen children in the world,"* and California as being *"the largest market for stolen children in the United States,"* and yet our State Department invited NO *adoptee* groups to participate. Instead of going through the State Department, I wrote directly to Vitit Muntharborn, then Special Rapporteur to the United Nations Economic and Social Council, Commission on Human Rights, explaining the extent of my involvement with adoption, and families dismembered by adoption, and offered data with regard to black market and "legalized" adoption and child trafficking.

Muntharborn welcomed the news articles, data with sources, and other input that showed how methods for procuring children, for a variety of illicit purposes from sweatshop work to child sex trafficking, is enhanced by sealed records laws, falsified birth records, and the lack of Immigration's monitoring of children who were being taken OUT of the country allegedly for adoptions abroad. Nevertheless the U.N. chose "diplomacy" over "rights" when it decided that it was okay for Americans to literally kidnap children from third world countries, then "legally" adopt them in the United States *under color of state sealed records statutes "if in child's best interests"* – that vague term that keeps popping up in courts and agencies that use the phrase *to justify Government Protected Child Stealing from parents who are not unfit.*

September 30, 1992

AMERICANS FOR OPEN RECORDS(AmFOR)
PO Box 401, Palm Desert, CA 92261
U.S.A.

ATT: VITIT MUNTARBHORN, Special Rapporteur,
  UNITED NATIONS CENTRE FOR HUMAN RIGHTS
  J.H.A. van LOON, First Secretary,
  HAGUE CONFERENCE ON PRIVATE INTERNATIONAL ADOPTION LAW
  PETER PFUND, US Legal Advisor, U.S. STATE DEPARTMENT
  ORLAN PRESTEGARD, Chair, Draft Model Adoption Act Committee,
  UNIFORM STATE LAWS COMMISSION
  CONGRESSWOMAN PAT SCHROEDER, Chair,
  SELECT COMMITTEE ON CHILDREN, YOUTH & FAMILIES
  CONNECTICUT STATE JUDICIARY CHAIRMAN TULISANO & Committee Members
  CALIFORNIA GOVERNOR PETE WILSON (as response to SB-1148)
  ALL STATE JUDICIARY CHAIRS
  AMERICANS FOR OPEN RECORDS (AmFOR) network
  (enclosure: American Journal of Adoption Reform, Sept. 21, 1992)

PROPOSAL

As an international adoption civil liberties network serving as data
source to the United Nations and Hague Conference projects on Rights of
the Child (Adoption), AMERICANS FOR OPEN RECORDS proposes the following:

BECAUSE the United Nations has identified the United States of America
as the largest marketplace of children in the world, and because, on
July 16, 1991, Romanian President Iliescu signed a new adoption law
which is helping to stop the Romanian baby trade, we propose that
nations, including the United States, "adopt" a version of the Romanian
law as a "universal model" toward eliminating the "need" for adoption.
The following was published in Feminist Studies, Volume 18, No 2,
Summer 1992:

"Among the (1992 Romanian) law's provisions is the necessary
institutionalization of orphaned children. This is meant to prevent
sale of children and to determine the legal status of children as
orphans. (Children must literally be orphaned or abandoned; if they
are under the care of a parent, then they are not legally adoptable.)
Children must reside in an orphanage for six months, during which time
the natural parents may change their minds, or adoptive parents may
(then) be found among Romanian citizens. Only thereafter are foreigners
eligible to adopt Romanian children."

CONSIDER that 99% of Americans "orphans" from 1950 through 1992 have not
been "true orphans" but "economic orphans" whose natural parents were
coerced into so-called "voluntary" relinquishments of parental rights
"in the child's best interests" under parens patriae -- state adoption
laws which deprive adoption affected parties of basic civil rights,
including due process, as a "legitimate state interest in protecting its
citizens." Such protection has been neither humanitarian nor cost
effective in the long run, as most of the states are now required to
provide post-adoption services, including intermediary counseling and
registry of adoptees and birth parents seeking information and contact
with one another, as well as tedious and expensive searches to locate
the parties after as many as 18 or more years of forced separation.

101

State and national response to judicial challenges to past and present adoption practices has been an attempt to further reduce the parties' ability to challenge the validity of such relinquishments and adoptions. In California, SB-1148 proposes signed "waivers" nullifying due process rights in exchange for notification of one's "rights" by adoption facilitators with a vested interest in consummating relinquishments. Well publicized studies have determined that children, who are perhaps materially advantaged by stranger adoptions, are at the same time more likely to become societal problems from emotional injury that statutory secrecy and severance of kinship ties inflicts. Make adoption the "last resort" or the human toll, and therefore the cost to the state and the nation, will be the nation's downfall.

CONSIDER that the United States still has no adoption data collection system as Congress authorized back in 1988 but cannot seem to find the funds to implement it. CONSIDER, TOO, that we have no idea just how many American children leave the country to be adopted abroad or to become another of the Justice Department's unpublished "missing children" statistics; a child sells for $50,000 ("street value") for every imaginable purpose. Kiplinger magazine cites the "average private adoption now costs $25,000" and the demand for adoptable (white) babies is at an all time high in the U.S. Legally falsified, sealed adoption birth records in the U.S. has covered up mass child stealing rings since the 1950's. (Reference Tennessee Children's Home Society and "The Woman Who Stole 5,000 babies; 1992 Thacker case; there are thousands of these.) Uniform, true birth records can easily halt much of today's international and insterstate baby trafficking, yet commissions and committees resist this simple measure for fear that future safegards will prompt opening a proverbial "can of worms" and reveal extensive government protected child stealing in the past, as many now-adult adoptees and their birth parents discover as result of locating one another years later despite statutory obstacles. One federal case in Connecticut, by a birth mother and an adoptee, has overcome the statute of limitations and seeks to overcome immunity of state officials from wrongful adoption suits; adoption fraud suits by adoptive parents now flood state courts nationwide.

The Feminist Studies article goes on to say that "...Romania has embraced the principles of Article 21 of the United Nations Convention on The Rights of the Child; it has also unwittingly endorsed a feminist measure. This law will help to alleviate the abuse suffered by those women coerced into giving up their children." Any violation of human rights impacts not only on women and children; universal adoption scandals are not just a feminist issue. How a nation treats its citizens impacts on every citizen. Therefore, AmFOR urges all states and nations to draft and enact truly equitable policy based on the Romanian model and to reform its institutionalized child and family services

Respectfully,

Lorraine Carangelo

LORRAINE CARANGELO
Executive Director

AMERICANS FOR OPEN RECORDS(AmFOR)
PO Box 401, Palm Desert, CA 92261

10 July 1992
Original: ENGLISH

RIGHTS OF THE CHILD

Sale of Children
in the United States of America

A Special Report to the United Nations
Economic and Social Council, Commission on Human Rights
Special Rapporteur, Mr. Vitit Muntarbhorn,
in accordance with Commission resolution 1990/68

submitted by
AMERICANS FOR OPEN RECORDS (AmFOR)
Lorraine Carangelo, Executive Director
76-670 Thrush #1, P.O. Box 401
Palm Desert, California 92261
U.S.A.

AMERICANS FOR OPEN RECORDS (AmFOR) is grateful to the following individuals for their contribution of information and material for this project:

EUGENE AUSTIN
prime mover for enactment of Parental Kidnap Prevention
and Uniform Custody,
lay researcher to prosecutors,
national and international networker, lobbyist for family law reforms,
and former organizer of fathers'and mothers'"undergrounds"
to save abused, government kidnapped children
104 East 3rd Street, P.O. Box 115
Tilden, Nebraska 68781
U.S.A.

MARY LOUISE FOESS
public school teacher, national adoption reform lobbyist,
lay researcher and writer on adoption issues,
and founder-president of adoption search-support organization
BONDING BY BLOOD, UNLIMITED
4710 Cottrell Road, RR 5
Vassar, Michigan 48768
U.S.A.

RICKIE SOLINGER
Visiting Scholar in Women's Studies at the University of Colorado,
Associate of the Rocky Mountain Women's Institute,
and author of
"Wake Up Little Susie: Single Pregnancy and Race Before Roe v. Wade"
(for permission to include her book as support for this report)
1017 Maxwell
Boulder, Colorado 90304
U.S.A.

and also:

MARY IWANEK
co-author of paper detailing history of adoption
and disclosure of information experiences in other countries
which opened up adoption in New Zealand
14 Emerson Street
Petone
New Zealand

*****

TABLE OF CONTENTS

TABLE OF EXHIBITS

107

111

2. DONOR INSEMINATION, SURROGACY, OTHER NON-TRADITIONAL PARENTING

3. GENOCIDE BY ADOPTION

4. SALE OF CHILDREN FOR SEX AND PORNOGRAPHY

5. Child Labor in the United States

INTRODUCTION

1. Purpose. This report is to provide the Special Rapporteur with information and data concerning "<u>Sale of Children in the United States</u>," for his report on "<u>Sale of Children</u>."

2. Who we are. What we do. AMERICANS FOR OPEN RECORDS (AmFOR)[1] is an international voluntary civil liberties network concerned with violations of the rights of children and families as enumerated in the Universal Declaration of Human Rights. We are unfunded and unconflicted. Our primary focus has been adoption affected children and adults as represented by our informal international membership of adoption affected individuals and groups represented adoption affected individuals.

3. Sources. AmFOR has researched and compiled information on sale of children with emphasis on sale for adoption, with the help of networkers in all 50 states and 20 countries. For the purpose of this report and the material supporting it, it is impractical to identify and credit every individual and properly thank each; the 4 individuals who contributed the most research and material, identified on the previous page, represent many others. Where possible, sources are noted for every statistic, newsclipping and article and other support material with this report.

A. General Considerations

4. Politicizing of families, the child and the courts as contributing factors.
The phenomena of the sale of children is rampant in the United States which is described by the Special Rapporteur as the largest marketplace for children. We attribute this to America's "supply and demand" economy which has led to corruption and abuse including exploitation and commoditization of America's children and of the world's children by Americans.

While the Special Rapporteur presents a global picture of developed countries robbing the developing countries of their children--for adoption and for every imaginable use of children--and sees the underlying motive as financial profit, other motives are alluded to, such as free or cheap labor, population control, politicizing children's rights based on their poverty, or genocide. But in the United States, post-World War II, the white baby of the unwed mother in particular became a valuable commodity connected to politics of race, as explained and chronicled in "Wake Up Little Susie" by Rickie Solinger.[2] That book has been photocopied and provided as support for this report by permission of its author. The book documents unwed pregnancy and race as intertwined issues before <u>Roe v. Wade</u>, the famous U.S. Supreme Court abortion ruling.

Government protected child stealing is made easy by statutory falsification and sealing (in state courts)[5] of the pre-adoption and post-adoption birth and adoption records. Adoption-related crimes are easily swept under the seal. When one of the United States is the "receiving state" for foreign born children whose adoptions are finaled here, or who are "re-adopted" here, the foreign born child's origins are obliterated by the "legal fiction" that the child is "born to" his adopters. Baby borkers, including adoption lawyers, physicians and other "middlemen" often admit pregnant women to hospitals for delivery of their babies under the name of the prospective adopter, often without the birth mother's knowledge, as the children later learn when they search out their birth mothers, and as documented by adoption search groups in the United States and Canada. The Hague International Adoption Treaty convention has yet to define "adoption" and addresses access to true birth records only by refernce to the "controlling statute of the receiving state." No state in the United States has uniform adoption and records access laws.

5. **Right to know.** One of the most basic needs for which there is an innate quest for satisfaction is the adoptee's basic need or right to knowhis origins--his true heritage. The Universal Declaration of Human Rights, Article 15, part 1, states: "Everyone has the right to his own nationality" and (in part 2) "No one shall be arbitrarily deprived of his nationality nor denied the right to change his nationality." The United States Supreme Court, struggling with the abortion issue, on June 29, 1992 ruled that the states may restrict access to abortion unless "undue burden" is shown. "Undue burden" is a vague term similar to the "good cause" requirement in most states which precludes anyone from opening an adoption record. Anti-abortion activists promote adoption as a preventative to abortion, yet the adoption reform movement cites that abortions are usually the option women choose over the pain of surrendering a live child to an unknown destiny in the hands of strangers in secret adoptions. The baby in the famous Roe v. Wade case was not aborted; the mother was forced to relinquish the baby girl for secret adoption by strangers. The courts have held that depriving the class of adoption affected citizens of basic Constitutional rights, including due process and equal protection, is a "legitimate state interest"--that the state's imposition of secrecy is to "protect the integrity of the institution of adoption" -- regardless of whether it injures the adopted child and all parties to an adoption and regardless of whether adoption related crimes are enhanced by such "protection." Similar arguments to those on behalf of Black Americans who were slaves at the time of our civil war and abolition of slavery toward civil rights acts a century later are argued on behalf of adopted children today. Involuntary servitude by adoption was known in ancient times, but in the United States, there was no secrecy component to adoption for the first 200 years of our history (and "nothing awful" happened). New Deal social welfare programs were met with government protected kidnap schemes, statutes and policies in the 1940's and 1950's. The 1950's and 1960's saw an escalation of demand for white adoptable children by design. The shorter the supply the further Americans will travel to find children in other countries and the more unconstitutional are the custody decisions and lawmaking to expedite child stealing. The current case of "Baby Angelica" who was returned to her natural (unwed) mother aroused the nation in support of the foster parents who wanted to adopt the baby despite that the natural mother had never consented to an adoption. The unwed mother has become a scapegoat for political plundering of the economy and is seen as a welfare burden, while a multi-billion dollar adoption industry provides tax breaks, subsidies and services to adopters that working poor and middle class mothers do not qualify for. The working poor and middle class parents end up paying taxes to subsidize middle class infertile couples to adopt their children. But also it is not unsual to place a child from an unwed or married natural parent with a single adoptive parent of higher income or material advantage or "political correctness," in much the same mindset as the forced German adoptions. Discretionary decisions by state and private adoption facilitators are usually rubber stamped by the courts or, as in the case of Baby Angelica,[4] state social services will appeal a court's return of a child to its natural parent.

6. **Clear and present danger.** We, in the anti-adoption movement, find that three generations of a family, each generation dismembered by the state for adoption, is becoming the norm and so the main focus of this report is on Sale For Adoption,

B. Methodology

7. Five areas of concern. AmFOR's report examines five specific areas of concern under the title <u>Sale of Children in the United States</u>. Four of the five subjects overlap with adoption since the practice or prohibition is enhanced by statutory adoption secrecy. They are:

> (1) sale of children for adoption, and
> adoption for commercial purposes;
>
> (2) donor insemination and surrogacy cases;
>
> (3) sale of children for sex, pornography;
>
> (4) racial genocide and experimentation by adoption;

Because I happened to have some newsclips and data on child labor in the United States, from colonial white slavery and indenture[5] to current child labor practices[6] (which seem to be on the increase due to our present economic problems). I have enluded:

> (5) child labor in the United States.

The brief summaries of the report are supported by the enclosed studies, newsclippings, statistical or anecdotal data and prosecuted or pending cases.

8. Method of work. The method of work was based upon:

> 1. documentation on past and current cases or studies obtained by AmFOR since its January 1, 1989 founding through the present time; some of the material covers samplings over several years to document historical trends and politics leading to current practice; other documents are examples of a singular event or is typical of many identical situations nationwide and/or internationally;
>
> 2. AmFOR's direct involvement with some of the cases or persons reported on or publicized in support material with the report;
>
> 3. input from thousands of individuals in the 50 states and 20 countries (as listed herein) who contacted AmFOR.

THE SUPPORT DOCUMENTATION FOR EACH OF THE FIVE (5) CATEGORIES, ABOVE, ACCOMPANIES THIS REPORT IN FIVE (5) SECTIONS LABELED WITH THE CAPTIONS IN NUMBERS 1 THROUGH 5, AS ABOVE. Footnotes in the report refer to the specific sections and page numbers within the section.

SALE OF CHILDREN IN THE UNITED STATES

9. **Defining "child" and "sale."** The Convention on the Rights of the Child defines "child" as "every human being below the age of 18, <u>unless, under the law applicable to the child</u>, majority is attained earlier." The Convention apparently is not planning to assess whether "the law applicable to the child" which defines "child" is, in fact, in keeping with the intent of the Universal Declaration of Human Rights. AmFOR believes it is important that a universal definition of "child" be addressed; otherwise the "applicable laws" of states may continue to violate children's rights by simply categorizing or defining human beings whose rights are violated by the state as "forever a child" (as in adoption) or by postponement of "age of majority" statutorily.[7] In the 50 states, for instance, there is no uniform "age of majority." Each of the United States has its own statutory "age of majority" for specific privileges and obligations of citizens within the state. In California, the "age of majority" is 18 for obtaining a driver's license, to vote, to apply for a marriage license, and to be served alcohol. Contract law allows that a "minor," below the age of 18, may not be held to his contract as it is "voidable." But also, in California,[8] an "adopted child" may not access true adoption birth records or information about himself until age 21. In Nebraska,[9] the adoptee is an "adopted child" for the purpose of accessing information until age 25. In Kansas,[10] Alaska[11] and Alabama,[12] the "adult adoptee" (age 18) may obtain his pre-adoption (unfalsified) birth certificate from the vital records office without an intermediary review and decision. In California, even if the adoptee "over 18," complies with conditions for access, unless his birth mother also registers for such access, the adoptee will be denied. (Until this year, the "adult adoptee's" adoptive parent also was required to register permission.) In Connecticut, even after birth parent and adult adoptee "register" their consents to release information about themselves to one another, the adoptee is required to undergo psychiatric evaluation as to his "ability to receive the information." In most states that have "registries," intermediary systems or other statutory provisions for such access, the court or agency still has final discretion over whether such access will be permitted (the test of "good cause"). (Note that many states have <u>no</u> provisions for access at all and courts refuse.) On June 29, 1992, the U.S. Supreme Court ruled that Pennsylvania may apply its statutory restrictions on legal abortions, unless "undue burden" is proven. In adoption, "undue burden" is often an "impossible burden" for adoptees and their biological parents attempting to access information and records, since there is no ruling or statutory definition as to what constitute's "undue burden." Again, it's left to the discretion of uninvolved parties and courts and each agency or court in each district may subscribe to a different interpretation.

Americans hold as diverse interpretation of the term "sale" with regard to sale of children as they do with regard to the term "child." Courts and legislatures have struggled with "amounts paid" and to whom paid in deciding whether an adoption is actually a "sale." "The Book of Insider Information" by Boardroom Classics, a New York publisher, in an article titled "Baby Shortage: Adoption Strategies" (which is an attachment to this report)[13] suggests a guideline that "Expenses of $5,000 to $7,000 are reasonable. Payments in the range of $20,000 to $40,000 leave you open to a charge of child-buying." Yet $8,000 to $40,000 is not an unusual amount for an adoption lawyer or baby broker, "matching center" or private adoption agency to charge adopters. Most of the money is pocketed by the facilitator.

AmFOR's policy statement declares that "there is a sale in every adoption" since adoption affected citizens lose their civil and human rights in the transfer of parental rights.

117

10. History of adoption and adoption secrecy laws. Perhaps the most comprehensive report on the history of adoption and adoption secrecy laws was researched
and compiled by Mary Iwanek from New Zealand. That report is an attachment to
this report as further support.[+]

11. Slavery. The report by the Special Rapporteur addresses "slavery." It
is worthwhile to note that black African slaves as well as white slaves whose
free, forced labor helped build this country, were subjected to name changes to
obliterate kinship ties through identity. In the same way, American adoptees'
names are changed upon adoption and a new, falsified birth certificate is issued
"as if born to" their adopters on the same date of their true birth, to deny
existence of or past relationship to biological relatives. A detailed account of
white slavery in early America and indenture of children is an attachment to this
report titled "They Were White And They Were Slaves."[5] White slavery is virtually
unknown to the most avid student of American history since mention of it is
excluded from textbooks. In this report, child labor is combined with
slavery of the past and current child labor scandals and detailed in the last
section of this report - "5. Child Labor in the United States."

12. Mass geopolitical child stealing. Mr. Eugene Austin's incredible piece of
research titled "Geopolitical Mass Child Stealing"is incorporated with the "history,
and slavery material because it serves as the best summarized chronology-wit:-
sources in support of this report; Austin's 4-page report[6] is therefore an attachment.

1. SALE OF CHILDREN FOR ADOPTION; ADOPTION FOR COMMERCIAL PURPOSES.
In American legal precedent, it is assumed that the adopted child will have
automatic succession to inherit from his adopters "as if born to them" according
to the state of residence or state law controlling the estate. It is also assumed
that no adoptee in any state will inherit from his biological parents because the
biological parents are usually prevented from accessing their child's post-adoption
identity in order to name them in their wills. Unlike the ancients and royalty and
nobility of Britain and other countries, Americans were not so obsessed with
"producing an heir" as the courts were obsesssed with preventing illegitimates
from establishing legal claims of inheritance. Yet there are now precedents
established by adoptees who challenged their biological parents' estates and won,
as well as cases of adoptive parents disinheriting their children. (Example:
Cathy Yvonne Stone, illegitimate daughter of Country Western singer, the late
Hank Williams, in Stone v. Williams, won her claim on her father's estate despite
the statute of limitations, because the court decided she had not "sat on her rights"
since she did not know who her biolgical parents were because her records were
sealed. On the other hand, the late Joan Crawford, Hollywood actress for several
decades, disinherited all four of her adopted children, plus a child she had
briefly adopted and was forced to return to the birth mother.) So "money" may be
said to motivate the "public interest" in adoption, in fact and theory, and "money"
is the underlying reason for the "state's legitimate interest" in "protecting the
integrity of the adoption process," even where little or no money changes hands
in facilitating the adoption. Money is more obviously the motivating factor with
regard to present day American adoption practice as previously cited in "9. Defining 'child' and 'sale.'" Most state sealed records laws regarding adoptions were
passed by state legislatures just after President Franklin D. Roosevelt's "New
Deal" social welfare programs were enacted, which would support unwed moms and kids.

"Sale of children for adoption" has been documented in the United States and is on the rise. Baby want-ads in every major American newspaper evidence the commercialization of American adoption; children are "showcased" on television talk shows, including The Donahue Show, Geraldo and others, which appeal to viewers to apply to adopt those children shown on the program or "children like them." Catalogs of "adoptable children" with their photos and biographies are circulated by adoption agencies as well as "matching centers"unlicensed as adoption agencies, including The Independent Adoption Center, Pleasant Hill, California, which provides prospective adopters' "resumes" to birth parents to induce them to "select" new parents for their children and which gives preference to volunteer workers at the "matching center" as to "first choice" of babies and children that become available. IAC also receives grants to produce their "catalogs" and uses USA Today, a national Gannett newspaper, to run its baby want-ads, nationwide. IAC receives from $8,000 to $40,000, or more, per adoption.

a. **Abductions (random) and pre-selected kidnappings for adoption.**
Several examples of random abductions and pre-selected kidnappings are evidenced by the attachments to this report.[7] The latest trend is abductors or kidnappers posing as state officials--social workers, Protective Services authorities, etc.--to compel new parents to hand over their newborns. The general public has no way of knowing what constitutes valid identification of Social Service workers, how far their authority extends, as it differs from state to state, and even from county to county. Again, the "undue burden" of proving parental fitness rests upon the parent and there is no adequate "due process" for parents, or children involuntarily or voluntarily surrendered to the foster care system under Child Welfare Dept., and the Department's authority and actions was seldom questioned until recent scandals about child deaths and child molestations while in foster care surfaced in California, Connecticut, Florida and elsewhere.

b. **Hospital baby switches, snatches.**
Examples of hospital baby switches to obtain a child for adoption are attachments.[18] The best example is the Twigg case in Florida. Note that if any time goes by before an abducted or kidnapped child is found to be adopted, the courts will not order return of the child to his rightful parents, alleging it's "In the child's best interests" to remain in the home it is now familiar with, and with the parents it now knows, despite that a crime was committed in obtaining the child. The hospital "snatches" (where no second baby is switched for the stolen baby) are increasing as "copy cat" kidnappers pose as state officials and walk right into hospital rooms and easily induce new mothers to hand over their newborns. Still a prime target is the unwed mother whose physician (in the 1950's, 60's and today) tells her "the baby died" in order to take it for black market adoption. Long a practice of Canadian physicians as well, the stolen children may be on either side of the border.

c. **Institutional mass child stealing.**
False allegations of abuse and neglect are another plague resulting in loss of parental rights without due process, and wrongful adoption. Birth mothers are required by some doctors, hospitals, and baby brokers, to enter the hospital under the adopter's name to deliver the baby. There is then no record whatsoever of the biological parents. Indian child abductions, continuing today, are a classic example of institutional mass child stealing from America's beginnings, onward, as the Little Moon case and other examples, attached to report, evidence.[19]

119

writing proposes increasing rights of adopters and removing rights of biological parents. One group's critique of the current Draft Act is an attachment to this report.[26]

i. **Bush Administration's escalation of the "adoption option" through subsidy, manipulated/false data and underreporting.**
President Bush's "White House Memo No. 906627, Administrative Support For The Adoption Option"[27]paved the way for a $30-million dollar "Adoption Opportunities Act," a $1.2-billion dollar Federal Child.Welfare budget devoted mostly to adoption and foster care reimbursements to the states, and for tax breaks, subsidies and adoption-related services to adopters (designed to escalate adoptions) while no such subsidies or services are available to working poor and middle class parents struggling to keep and raise their children in today's recession/depression economy. Clearly the "adoption option" politics is intended to benefit the monied classes.and to alleviate government's responsibility to poorer families.

j. **The Open Records Movement and The Anti-Adoption Movement.**
These two distinctly separatist yet overlapping movements in the United States, and worldwide, mainly seek to eliminate the pain reported by all parties known as the "adoption triad" or "adoption affected persons"-- both birth families and adoptive families affected by adoption. In the United States, Jean Paton, MA, MSW, age 83, founded The Open Records Movement in 1953 as result of her studies, which were the first of their kind, of adoption affected families. Herself an adoptee, Paton promotes the "adopt a family" concept and considers American adoption to be a form of colonialism. In the 1960's, Eugene Austin began serving as lay researcher and activist for family rights cases and causes, including the Parental Kidnap Prevention Act and has since joined the worldwide networking movement to reform or eliminate adoption and provides AmFOR as well, as prosecutors and others,with lay research and support. On January 1, 1989, AMERICANS FOR OPEN RECORDS (AmFOR) was founded by Lorraine Carangelo, as result of her 18 year search for her son stolen for adoption and their 1987 reunion[29]and subsequent networking with individuals and organizations in the 50 states and Canada. AmFOR now has members and networking supporters in the 50 states and in 20 countries. AmFOR is an unfunded, unconflicted, volunteer adoption civil liberties network. It is not connected to any adoption-related business or other business. AmFOR works to eliminate the "need" for adoption and advocates truer expressions of transferred custody such as legal guardianships with true, open records and open arrangements without intermediary control. AmFOR has provided lay research to lawyers and lawmakers,and maintained pro se lawsuits on the sealed adoption records issue, provided documentation to support other cases, and is presently serving as data source to the Hague International Adoption Treaty Convention.

k. **Controlled samplings, longitudinal studies, anecdotal studies.**
1. Injury to child, medical
2. Injury to child, psychiatric
3. Injury to child, physical, sexual abuse
A 3-page summarized "Statistics of Adoption" report with sources precedes studies and newsclips concerning the three categories on Injury to Child.[28]

2. **DONOR INSEMINATION, SURROGACY, OTHER NON-TRADITIONAL PARENTING**
   Examples attached to this report demonstrate how these categories
   relate to "Sale of Children;" includes genetic experimentation. [29]

3. **GENOCIDE BY ADOPTION**
   Article explaining the concept precedes specific cases in which true
   race and nationality of the adoptee is at issue with regard to the
   genocide issue. [30]

4. **SALE OF CHILDREN FOR SEX AND PORNOGRAPHY**
   Children, incuding adopted and foster children, have long been
   targets of child sex and pornography rings in the United States.
   The children used may be violated over a period of years in their
   schools, churches, neighborhoods. They are also used by national
   and international rings that transport the kids from state to state
   to service wealthy clientele, including high level public officials.
   In the <u>Franklin</u> Case, a Nebraska Grand Jury would not give credibility
   to teenagers' testimony of events that occurred, allegedly involving
   then-Vice President George Bush, but later private investigations by
   a former FBI agent,and lie detector tests and other testimony and
   evidence,corroborated these witnesses allegations. The story has been
   circulating in Australian newsletters, by a team of Italian television
   investigative journalists, in Italian magazine Avvenimenti, and in
   the South African Afrikans language newspaper Oosterlig. An American
   CIA psychiatrist now living in Omaha reportedly investigated now-
   President Bush on similar charges. That material is provided with
   this report,for what it is worth,to support that such child sex
   rings exist, regardless of the specific allegations against alleged
   participants.[31] Judges and Nebraska Grand Jury members were said to be
   such participants. International child sex and pornography rings find
   easy access to children in the United States and easy trafficking of
   American children out of the U.S.

5. **CHILD LABOR IN THE UNITED STATES**
   The cover article "Child Labor Skyrockets"[32]is from wire reports that
   include national data by the U.S. Department of Labor, National Child
   Labor Committee and National Institute for Occupational Safety and
   Health--the latter stating that such statistics are "the tip of the
   iceberg," because there is no system to collect data.

Footnotes

1. AmFOR; j. The Open Records Movement and the Anti-Adoption Movement, 313-312, 321, 322-330, 346-347.
2. Solinger. (4) Wake Up Little Susie: Unwed Pregnancy amd Race Before Roe v. Wade.
3. Statutory sealing of records, g. Non-uniform laws by state, 205-221, Uniform Laws Commission Draft Model Adoption Act, commentary, 222.
4. Baby Angelica, Attachment 1 to July 10, 1992 letter to Vitit Muntarbhorn, HOmeless Mom's Vitory is Big Loss for Childless Pair, and Attachment 3, Children Stolen From Unwed Mothers.
5. White slavery and indenture, 5. Child Labor in the United States, 610-634.
7. Age of Majority statutes, g. 205-221
8,9,10,11-Age of majority statutes, g. 205-221
12. Age of Majority statutes, g. 205-221
13. Baby Shortage: Adoption Strategies by Boardroom Classics, i. 238.
14. (10) History of Adoption and Adoption Secrecy Laws by Mary Iwanek.
15. 610-634
16. (12) Geopolitical Mass Child Stealing by Eugene Austin.
17. Abductions, a. 1-10.
18. b. Hospital baby switches, 11-25.
19. Little Moon case, Indian cases, 532, 535, 536-7, 538, 539-541
20. Adoption and American-Canadian court decisions, 172-176, 185
21 Mexico: Missing Children-A Mexico Connection f. 138-139.
22. Black Market Adoption, e. 110-127.
23. Inter-state, inter-country adoptions, 128-204
24. Statutes: g. 205-221
25. Carangelo et al v. O'Neill et al, Attachment to July 10, 1992 letter to Vitit Muntarbhorn (Attachments 1, 2 pages).
26. Draft Model Adoption Act (commentary) h. 222.
27. White House Memo No. 906627 "Administrative Support for the Adoption Option" i (1.) 223-224.
28. (j.) 321, 326.
29. Injury to the child, k. 350-484.
30. 3. Genocide By Adoption, 527-597.
31. Franklin case   589-599, 600-608
31.   Child Labor Skyrockets (last section)

122

J.H.A. ("Hans") Van Loon
Former Secretary General of the Hague Conference
on Private International Law
"Mr. Van Loon noted that in order for the trafficking to succeed,
*it is essential that the child leave the country of origin
in a legal or **'seemingly legal'** way."* (1990 Report on Intercountry Adoption)

David M. Smolin, Professor of Law –
Cumberland School of Law, Birmingham, Alabama

"...the current intercountry adoption system frequently takes children ***illegally*** from birth parents, and then uses the official processes of the adoption and legal systems to ***'launder'*** them as *'legally'* adopted children. Reform international adoption, by putting a priority on keeping children in their original family and within their community...
14 1. A central authority, accredited adoption agencies and an inter-country adoption system under domestic laws and The Hague Convention *will not suffice to prevent child trafficking*."

1992- AmFOR and Hague Intercountry Adoption Treaty Conference

For the past five decades, children *illegally procured or kidnapped* in the United States have also been *"legally"* adopted under state adoption secrecy laws. The verbatim December 1992 Memo, below, was the U.S. State Department's legal opinion regarding *legalizing adoptions of children illegally procured or kidnapped.* In 1992, Peter Pfund, the State Department's Legal Adviser, sent the Memo to the U.S. Delegation of adoption agencies to the Hague Intercountry Adoption Convention – and directly to Lori Carangelo, Americans For Open Records (AmFOR) *because the U.S. State Dept. would not approve adoptee and parent groups as Delegates, yet the White House later appointed 2 adopters as Delegates.* So the Hague's First Secretary, J.H.A. Van Loon, permitted Carangelo / AmFOR to be a "Data Source," reporting *directly* to Van Loon. AmFOR provided a Proposal to the U.N. "Rights of the Child" Project, *including 634 "Exhibits" supporting the need for open adoption records worldwide,* and also provided Van Loon with a copy of the Pfund Memo, which is follows:

December, 1992
HAGUE CONVENTION ON INTERCOUNTRY ADOPTION
U.S. Federal Implementing Legislation – Issues
-2- "DeHart has suggested that there may be only two legitimate grounds for non-recognition [by Congress ratifying the Intercountry Adoption Convention & Treaty:
(1) that the child was abducted from its biological parent(s); and
(2) the consent of the biological parent(s) was false or obtained by fraud. **Neither would nullify an adoption** made either abroad, or in the United States as receiving State, as contrary to public policy under the present wording of convention Article 22, unless recognition would also be contrary to the *child's best interest."*

-4- Preservation of Information Concerning the Child's Origin.
"Article 25, as presently worded, requires State parties to the convention to preserve "information concerning the child's origin" until the laws of both countries involved in international adoption have access to that information. Such access may only become possible *years or decades after an adoption takes place.* Many U.S. states have different provisions concerning preservation of such information. Such information is likely to be gathered mainly by countries of origin from which a child is adopted. In order for the United States to be able to comply with its obligations to other countries party to the convention under Article 25 to preserve such information, the federal legislation may need *to impose a uniform preservation obligation throughout the United States. Federal legislation would presumably not impose any requirements for access, which would be left for the individual states of the United States to set."*

> ---Peter Pfund, Assistant Legal Adviser
> for Private International Law,
> U.S. Department of State (12/92 Memo)

DRAFT 1:   COMMENTS BY THE EXPERTS FROM THE UNITED STATES
REPRESENTING ADOPTION AFFECTED CITIZENS OF U.S. & FOREIGN ADOPTIONS
WITH REGARD TO "PRELIMINARY DRAFT NO. 7" FOR THE 17th SESSION OF
THE MAY 10-29, 1993 HAGUE CONFERENCE ON INTERCOUNTRY ADOPTION

Mr. Chairman, Americans For Open Records, a voluntary international
adoption civil liberties organization composed of adoption affected
persons (many of whom are also adoption professionals) requests this
letter be made a part of the permanent record of the May 1993 session.
We note that California Attorney General Daniel Lungren's "written
suggestions" were included in he September 1992 Draft (Page 50, footnote
33) and the Expert From Egypt makes a valid point (letter appended to
September 1992 Draft) concerning nations that do not accept adoption.
We provide yet another view which should also be addressed. The issues
raised by this Conference are more explosive than those of any other
treaty. At least one faction in Holland has begun inciting violence
in the United States (See Attachment 1, tape) from human rights violations where non-uniform statutes in the 50 states prevail over adoption
or re-adoption in any of the states. While the Hague Conference may
properly avoid opposing laws of any one nation, the September Draft
nevertheless tends to endorse certain practices in the United States
which violate the Universal Declaration of Human Rights under "parens
patriae" (state's interest). Where do reformists look for an international "model" if such model is merely a diplomatic compromise?

(1) Defining "adoption."
Mr. Chairman, the Draft indicates the Convention's intention to define
"adoption" at the May 1993 session. In the meantime, the Draft, like an
army of blind men attempting to describe an elephant from its diverse
parts, attempts to analyze adoption by its many complexities without
benefit of a definition of "adoption."   Such definition necessitates a
confrontation with the Universal Declaration of Human Rights, including
but not limited to, Article 15 (right to nationality), Article 25 (2)
(all children, whether born in and out of wedlock, shall enjoy the same
social protection), and Article 30 (no state may destroy such rights).
(See Attachment 2, on adoptees' dual citizenship). International adoptions have generally treated the child as a commodity. The Draft recognizes adoption as a "last resort" but why adoption? (See Attachment 3
on "SOS Moms." Austrian model.) The Draft's many "compromises" tend to
conflict with human rights law rather than serve as a neutral interpretation of adoption under human rights law which we suggest be addressed.

(2) The mythical "heavily damaged birth mother" (Draft pg. 144, #299)
"Although admitting the right of the child to obtain information about
his or her origins, the Special Commission understood that unrestricted
access would be unacceptable....some participants representing states of
origin stressed the inconvenience of recognizing unlimited right of
information in certain cases, e.g. when an unmarried mother has consented to the adoption of her child and years later is heavily damaged by
the disclosure of her past at a time when she may be happily married.
American history records that the "bastard child" was an undesirable and
his white middle class unwed mother was judged "mentally ill" for having
conceived and borne a child out of wedlock until the late 1950's and
early 1960's when hundreds of thousands of such "mentally ill" mothers
had to be explained. White Christian authority decided the mothers were
"rehabilitatable" if they surrendered their children to secret adoption.

125

by white middle class infertile married couples who then created a
demand for the appropriatable bastard child.("Wake Up Little Susie:
Single Pregnancy and Race Before Roe v. Wade" by Rickie Solinger;
Routledge,Chapman, Hall, NYC and Routledge, London, 1992, ISBN 0-415-
90448-X, an exhibit to AmFOR's Report on Sale of Children for Adoption
in the United States, "Right of the Child" project, United Nations.)
To insure workability of such a plan, secrecy of birth records statutes
were enacted in secret--not by a vote of the people and not according to
the desires or human rights of either mother, father or child. Never
has my government permited me, a birth mother, nor any party to an
adoption, a choice concerning disclosure from the begining. Even in
the few states which permit so-called "open adoption," the pre-adoption
birth certificate is falisfied and sealed against the wishes of the
involved parties who then may not have access to records in which they
are named, for life. Although my son and I circumvented state law and
reunited in 1987 when he was then an adult, the state still prohibits
us from viewing the documents by which we are bound. The United
States District Court of Connecticut, in 1992, upheld the "state's
interest" in violating our civil rights in Carangelo/Schafrick v.
v. O'Neill, State of Connecticut et al, H-90-21 EBB, which we are
appealing. The Federal Constitutional Court at Karlsruhe, Germany, on
1/31/89, ruled that "The common individual right encompasses also the
right to knowledge of one's own heritage" and illegitimacy is not
justification for violation of such right.

Mr. Chairman, it is our experience in facilitating thousands of reunions
between adult adoptees and birth parents that only 1% of birth parents
refused contact but none refused disclosure of information. No mother
forgets a child she has borne and we want to know if our children are
alive and well. No adoptee has ever refused disclosure or contact. The
1% of those birth mothers encouraged to keep their "family secret" must
not be cited as justification for violating human rights of adoptees and
birth parents worldwide, especially as that 1% were forced into secrecy;
if the Conference decides to uphold human rights, records must be open
from the start, thus preventing "damaged birth mothers" years later.

This Conference states its purpose is to (indirectly) prevent abduction,
sale and trafficking of children. Imposing one nation's secrecy policies
upon other nations through re-adoption under state law is the greatest
single factor enabling child adoption, sale and trafficking to flourish
and prevents accountability for coercive and fraudulent relinquishments.
The Draft recognizes that abuses more often result from independent or
private adoptions yet recognizes that all international adoptions are
eventually finalized by a Central Authority to minimize abuse. In fact,
however, at this moment, a private "arranger" is bringing Russian
children to Hawaii for medical treatment to make them "adoptable" in
California through a New Mexico private agency--the adoptions having
been finalized in Russia; the adopters pay the New Mexico an up-front
fee of $9,000 but there are undisclosed fees in Russia which raises
the cost to $20,000 (See Attachment 4, European Adoption Consultants Inc
itemization of fees for Russian adoption). And no one knows what deals
are made behind closed doors when physicians and lawyers "arrange"
international adoptions later finalized by a Central Authority.

Mr. Chairman, the Convention's good intention concerning "collecting,
maintaining and preserving" a child's records is lost on any nation bent
on appropriating the child's origins in conflict with the Universal
Declaration of Human Rights.

126

2016 - LGBT and THE "RIGHT TO ADOPT" – A THIRD VIEW

In 2016, a "right to adopt" theory was advanced by openly gay ACLU Director, Anthony D. Romero, in mailings of a survey intended to support same sex marriage. Romero never replied to my request for clarification on what appeared to be ACLU's endorsement of *adoption as a "right"* accrued from the right to marry.

While it is imperative that LGBT individuals in America be afforded access to the *"same* playing field" with the *"same* rights," as other Americans, it is a slap in the face of ALL adoptees to allege that *any* American has a *"right to adopt,"* when adoptees are stripped of basic *rights* similar to pre-Civil War slaves, via bastardizing and sealing of their origins and true birth records withheld from them even in adulthood – with the blessings of ACLU.

This *"right to adopt"* view possibly began with a 2007 poll by CNN and Opinion Research Corporation which found that 57% of respondents felt same-sex couples should have the *"right to adopt"* and 40% that they should not. Adoption by same-sex couples was legal in 22 states. 14 countries, and some territories *("LGBT Adoption,"* Wikipedia, 2014)

My "Third View," is that *no one* has a *"right"* to adopt someone else's child. The "right to marry" does not beget a *"right" to adopt*. Activists for LGBT rights need to respect millions of adoptees by refraining from suggesting a *"right to adopt."*

All adoptions result in an adoptee having *"**less rights**"* than a person raised by his/her biological parents (or *"**different rights**"* in the case of Native American adoptees, as claimed in former Executive Director of Arizona ACLU, Louis Rhodes, in his 7-7-92 letter responding to adoptee, Wes Bikoff). It is therefore extremely important that no artificial *"right" to adopt* be afforded any individual or couple for socio-political advantage or for any reason.

My position, which is neither an anti-LGBT view, nor an "anti-adoption" view, relies on the fact that while adults have a right to *choose* whether to marry, while *a minor child has "no choice" whether to be adopted nor by whom.*

By 2012, according to Wikipedia, approximately 2 million children in the United States were being raised by LGBT parents but were unable to establish a "legal relationship" with their LGBT parents. Two years prior, in 2010, a consensus developed among the medical, psychological, and social welfare communities that children raised by gay and lesbian parents "are just as likely to be well-adjusted as those raised by heterosexual parents." And so, in 2010, the Third District Court of Appeal of the State of Florida was satisfied that the issue is so far beyond dispute that it would be irrational to hold otherwise, and stated: "the **best interests**" of children are not preserved by prohibiting homosexual adoption." ***"Not prohibiting"* someone from adopting, who is *not* unfit to parent, does not bestow a *"right to adopt."***

"Parents, Families and Friends of Lesbians and Gays (PFLAG)," supports the *right* of straight, lesbian, gay, bisexual and transgender individuals and couples "to be parents," regardless of their marital status, through biological relationships," and, when qualified, via *adoptive or foster relationships*." (PFLAG Board of Directors on February 12, 1995. Revised April 1, 2012).

Similarly, "Right To Life" lobbyists *misrepresent* that adoption is a "cure for abortion," which is refuted by statistics in *"The Adoption and Donor Conception Factbook."*

"Adoption Uncensored" is a compilation of 30 years of chronologically archived newsclips and letters on adoption issues, including letters from ALCU as to the conflict of interest when responding to adoptees seeking ACLU support for an "open records policy" because ACLU's attorney members represent foster care agencies *that facilitate adoptions*.

Shame on ACLU.

Chapter 4:
Government Protected Child Stealing *After Death*
2024 – The Early Death of my Son and Final Coverup

I resided in California most of my adult life and Tom had been raised in Connecticut since his 1969 adoption. My son was 18 when I finally found him in 1987 by paying $2100 cash to Jane Servadio, an "underground" searcher in Connecticut, who contacted me as result of the New Haven Register's front page story about my search for my son. I phoned his adoptive mother, Lois Schafrick before contacting him, out of respect to the woman who raised my son as her own. Her husband, William, an alcoholic, allegedly left Lois for another woman when Tom was 10, which is when a neighbor let it slip that he was adopted, a fact that his adoptive parents had never told him.

Lois was receptive at first, as she supported his need to know, and he and I went on to have a 30-year relationship, by my paying for our alternating cross-country visits that included his girlfriends and wives, and daughter. But despite that he would park in her driveway with me in his car, hoping she would meet me, she refused to do so. After four years of her refusals, I tried to force a face-to-face meeting with Lois, something I had always advised others against doing, at the Connecticut grocery store where she worked, in my belief that it would be good for him to have both his mothers on the same page. It must have been as much a shock for her, as it was for me, to see how The Children's Center had "matched" our physical appearance to enable the lie that she was his biological mother. Whether she believed that post-sealed adoption contact with me was illegal, or whether she was still upset over press coverage about the circumstances around the adoption, I don't know, but when I invited her to have lunch with me, or to meet after work, she screamed at me *"You knew I didn't want this – GET OUT or I'll have you arrested!"* Shaken by her anger and loudness, I could only manage to respond *"I'm sorry you feel that way. I'm here to pay his lawyer $2,000 to keep him out of jail"* to which she repeated her threat, so I left. Like most adoptees bound by loyalty and gratitude to their adopters, lest they, too, abandon them, Tom could not relate to me in a *"protective"* way, no matter what hurtful insults she had him repeat to me in between his "Love yous" over the years. If Lois had not already died in May 2023 at age 82, I assume she probably would not have notified me that I had again lost my son when he died on February 21, 2024 at age 55.

It was my son's former girlfriend who messaged me via my Facebook page, on March 16, 2024, twenty days after his death, and hours after she had attended his funeral service, *asking if I knew that my son had died.* She and Tom once stayed with me in California and although she and my son had remained friends, they had not had contact in several years. According to the Beecher and Bennett Funeral Home, it had fallen upon Tom's adoptive brother, James, to compose Tom's Obit. Opting to again "erase" me as Tom's "mother," James filled in their form stating that that my son was *"born to William and Lois Schafrick,"* with no mention of me among the relatives listed, perhaps out of respect for what I believe would have been Lois's need to maintain an "appearance of normalcy" that the love of *two* mothers might ruin for her. The Obit also claimed Tom had died from *"a sudden heart attack,"* but the photo used for the Obit revealed his "sunken eyes look" that Tom once called *"the face of a drug addict,"* and so I requested the Connecticut State Medical Examiner's findings as to his Cause of Death. Their letter-report stated the *primary* Cause of Death was *"Acute Fentanyl and Cocaine Intoxication"* and ruled it *"Accidental."*

James was born to Lois 8 years after they adopted my son. According to Tom, Lois and William Schafrick had been unable to get pregnant, so the Schafricks adopted in the belief that they could not otherwise have children. Tom was given the responsibility of taking care of his younger brother while his divorced mother worked. Tom told me and others he always felt that James was *"the favored son."* Tom's adoptive parents were blue collar workers, not well educated, and Tom dropped out of high school. James pursued higher education, and is employed in an administrative position in procurement at the Catholic college from which he graduated. I wondered whether James' gay identity was as much a "family secret" as my son's adoptive status was supposed to be. I assumed Lois was not only "protecting" herself, but also James, from contact with me. Having never been invited to meet James, I assume he found it too difficult to inform me my son had died. In adulthood, Tom and James had been estranged for a time, until Tom sent me photos taken at his brother's wedding when James was able to openly marry his husband.

After Tom's death, his former girlfriend and I spent several days exchanging information and photos to "fill in the blanks" -- the good, the sad, and the ugly, about the person we both cared for but who we did not know to the extent we thought we did. Even as I documented the emotional abuse suffered by *other* victims of sealed adoption that resulted in *their* drug and alcohol addictions and even suicides (as documented in *"The 8 Ball Café"*) I questioned my "not knowing," for years, that my own son was drug addicted, and my lack of tears, just anger, or whether anger is a form of grief, as I blamed my son's death on the lies and loyalties imposed by his sealed adoption, legislators, and courts, that robbed him of his identity, self worth, and the life he should have had. And I blamed myself for not trying harder to re-connect with my son before he died, other than expressing condolences when Lois died, hoping her loss would free him from the demands of her "unconditional" love.

Thomas W. Schafrick

December 17, 1968
~ February 21, 2024

Born in: New Haven, CT
Resided in: Meriden, CT

♥ Light a Candle

📁 Add a Memory to the Timeline

📖 Sign the Guestbook

Thomas William Schafrick, 55, of Meriden, passed away suddenly of cardiac arrest at his home on February 21, 2024. He was born on December 17, 1968, in New Haven, to William and Lois (Waller) Schafrick of Meriden.

A son, brother, friend, and father, Tommy has touched the lives of so many. Being self-employed, he spent a lot of time working, but all his free time was dedicated to being with Madison and Thomas, who meant the world to him.

He will be dearly missed by his son Thomas, daughters Madison, Rachel Molnar, and Rebecca Latham, his brother James Schafrick, brother-in-law Christopher Carlone, former wife Lisa Besek, many extended relatives

Tom's Obit

131

State of Connecticut
Office of the Chief Medical Examiner
11 Shuttle Road, Farmington, CT 06032
Telephone: (860) 679-3980

3/27/2024

Mother

Re: Medical Records Letter
M.E. Case Number 24-03949, Thomas William Schafrick
Date of Death: 02/21/2024

Dear Lori,

The examinations pertaining to the death of **Thomas William Schafrick** have been completed. The cause of death has been determined to be **Acute fentanyl and cocaine intoxication.** The other significant condition(s) contributing to the death included **Hypertensive and Atherosclerotic Cardiovascular Disease.** The manner of death has been determined to be **Accident**.

In accordance with the Administrative Regulations of the Commission of Medicolegal Investigations, copies of Medical Examiner's Office reports may be furnished to you upon payment of the fee indicated on the enclosed form. It has been our experience, because these are technical, medical documents that families often prefer to have the reports sent to a physician or an attorney. If you would like to have reports sent to someone other than yourself, please supply his/her name and address on the form.

If you have any questions concerning the examination, cause or manner of death, please contact Dr. James R. Gill, M.D. at (860) 679-3980.

Very truly yours,

James R. Gill, M.D.
Chief Medical Examiner

Connecticut State Medical Examiner's Actual Findings

Rest in Peace

BIBLIOGRAPHY

Akafate, Roman, *"International Adoption Corruption: What You Must Know   Before You Adopt a Child or Children,"* Amazon, 2015
    Armstrong, L., *"Of 'Sluts' and 'Bastards': A Feminist Decodes the Child Welfare Debate,"* Common Courage Press, 1995

Austin, Linda Tollet, *"Babies For Sale: The Tennessee Children's Home,"* Greenwood Press, 1993

Benet, Mary K., *"The Politics of Adoption,"* The Free Press, 1976

Bloom, Dr. Lee, *"Growing Up Behind Locked Doors,"* Rolling Stone Magazine, 1986

Borders, Anthony, *"Mother's 18-Year Search Ends,"* Press-Enterprise, 5-18-87

Bowlby, J., *"Illegitimacy and Deprivation,"* World Health Organization, Maternal Care and Mental Health, Monograph Series 4, 2nd ed. 115,149, 1952; and *"Childhood Mourning and Its Implications for Psychiatry,"* American Journal of Psychiatry, The Alfred Meyer Lecture, p.481-498, 1961

Brodzinsky, David M., Marshal Schecter and Robin Marantz Henig, *"Being Adopted: The Lifelong Search for Self,"* Anchor, 1993

Brown v. Board of Education, 347 US 473 (1952), *"Separate but equal violates the Constitutional right of Equal Protection."*

Cadoret, Remi J., "Biologic Perspectives of Adoptee Adjustment," in *"The Psychology of Adoption,"* (Brodzinsky), Oxford Press University, 1990

Carp, E. Wayne, *"Jean Paton and the Struggle to Reform American Adoption,"* University of Michigan Press, 2014; *"Adoption Politics: Bastard Nation and Ballot Initiative 58,"* University Press of Kansas, 2004

Chesler, Phyllis, *"Sacred Bond,"* and Mothers On Trial," 1986

Chronicle of Social Change, *"Cliff Notes on Family First Act, Part One: Services to Prevent Foster Care,"* 2-13-18

Coles, Gary, *"The Invisible Men of Adoption,"* BookPOD, 2011

D'Arcy, Claudia Corrigan, *"National Council For Adoption: Mothers, Money, Marketing and Madness,"* Musings of the Lame, 2007

DeCamp, John W, *"The Franklin Cover-Up: Child Abuse, Satanism and Murder in Nebraska,"* AWT Incorporated, 2011

Diver, Alice, *"A Law of Blood Ties: The Right to Access Genetic Ancestry,"* Springer Verlag, 2013

Donalds, Elizabeth S., *"Voices of Adoptees: Stories and Experiences Within the Schools,"* dissertation, Antioch University-New England, 2012

Fessler, Ann, *"The Girls Who Went Away,"* Penguin Books, 2007; and *"A Girl Like Her,"* [motion picture], LEF Foundation, Moving Image Fund, 2012

Fariris, Theresa Rodrigues, *"When Adoption Fails,"* Housekeeper Publishing, 2008

Fisher, Nancy L., MD, MPH, *"Cultural and Ethnic Diversity: A Guide for Genetics Professionals,"* John Hopkins University Press, 1966

Flango, Victor E. and Carol R., *"The Flow of Adoption Information from the States,"* National Center for State Laws, 1998

Goldstein, LA, AJ Solnit, *"Beyond the Best Interests of the Child,"* Free Press 1972

Goodman, Peter S., *"Stealing Babies for Adoption,"* Washington Post Foreign Service, 3-12-06

Griffith, Keith, *"The Right to Know Who You Are,"* Katherine Kimball, 1992

Hayes, John, *"Theft By Adoption,"* Lulu.com; Amazon Books (7-14-08)

Hentz, Trace Lara, *"Stolen Generations: Survivors of the Indian Adoption Projects and 60s Scoop,"* Blue Hand Books, 2016

Hood, G., *"Adoption or Abduction?"* Dan Rather Reports, AXS TV, 2012

Inglis, K., *"Living Mistakes: Mothers Who Consented to Adoption,"* G. Allen & Unwin, 1984

Janis, Chris, *"Mom Hopes Ad Will End Adoption Mystery,"* New Haven Register, 12-15-86

Jordheim, Alisa, *"Made In The USA: The Sex Trafficking of America's Children,"* Justice Society, 2015

Joyce, Kathryn, *"The Child Catcher: Rescue, Trafficking and the New Gospel of Adoption,"* PublicAffairs, 2013

Kirk, H. David, *"Shared Fate: A Theory of Adoption and Mental Health,"* The Free Press of Glencoe, 1994

Kirschner, David, PhD, *"Understanding Adoptees Who Kill: Dissociation, Parricide and the Psychodynamics of Adoption,"* Sage Journals, 2016; *"The Adopted Child Syndrome: Considerations for Psychotherapy,"* Psychotherapy In Private Practice, 1990; *"Son of Sam and the Adopted Child Syndrome,"* Adelphi Society, 1978; *"Adoption Forensics: The Connection Between Adoption and Murder,"* Crime Magazine, 2007

Lahl, Jennifer, *"Baby Market as Financial Market,* Center for Bioethics & Culture, 2016

Lawrence, M, *"The Demonized Mother,"* Lecture at First National American Adoption Congress, Washington, DC, M

Lechnit, Carroll, *"Bill, Suit Seek to Open Up All Adoption Files,"* Orange County Register, 4-29-90

Mahr, Christine, *"The Paper Chase for Birthparents,"* The Desert Sun, 2-17-90

Musser, Sandra K., *"To Prison With Love: An Indecent Indictment and America's Adoption Travesty,"* The Awareness Press, 2014

Rather, Dan, *"Adopted or Abducted?"* Dan Rather Reports, Richard Dawkins Foundation for Reason and Science, 2012

Reagan, Michael, *"On the Outside Looking In,"* Zebra, 1988

Riben, Marsha, *"Shedding Light on the Dark Side of Adoption,"* Harlo Press 1988

Richards, Cory L., *"The Adoption vs Abortion Myth,"* Reuters, 2013

Robinson, Evelyn Burns, *"Adoption and Loss: The Hidden Grief,"* Clova Publications, 2003; *"Adoption Should Be Abolished,"* Opposing Viewpoints

Roorda, Rhonda M., *"In Their Voices: Black Americans On Transracial Adoption," Columbia University Press,"* 2007

Rosenblatt, Katarline, *"Stolen: True Story of a Sex Trafficking Survivor,"* Aha Publishing, 2014

Samuels, Elizabeth, *"How Adoption in America Grew Secret,"* Washington Post, 2001

Sawyer, Josh, *"Death by Adoption,"* Cicada Press, 2014

Schecter, Marshall, *"Observations on Adopted Children,"* Archives of General Psychiatry, 1960; *"Emotional Problems in the Adoptee,"* Archives of General Psychiatry, 1964

Solinger, Rickie, *"Beggars and Choosers: How the Politics of Choice Shapes Adoption, Abortion and Welfare in the United States,"* Hill and Wang, 2001; *"Wake Up Little Susie: Single Pregnancy and Race Before Roe v. Wade,"* Routledge, 2000

Smolin, D., *"Child Laundering: How the Intercountry Adoption System Legitimizes and Incentives the Practices of Buying, Trafficking, Kidnapping, and Stealing Children"* Berkeley Electronic Press, 2005.

Thomas, Gordon, *"Enslaved: The Chilling Modern Day Story of Abandonment and Abuse in the Global Trafficking of Men, Women, Children,"* Pharos, 1991

Verhovek, Sam How, *"Public Lives: An Adoption Hero Who Knows All the Arguments,"* New York Times, 6-3-2000

Verrier, Nancy Newton, *"Primal Wound: Understanding the Adopted Child,"* Gateway Press, 2003

Walker, Leslie, *"A Sudden Fury," A True Story of Adoption and Murder,"* St. Martin's Press, 1989

Wellisch, E., *"Children Without Genealogy – A Problem of Adoption,"* Mental Health 13, 1952

Wilson-Buterbaugh, Karen, *"The Baby Scoop Era: Unwed Mothers, Infant Adoption and Forced Surrender,"* Amazon Books 2017

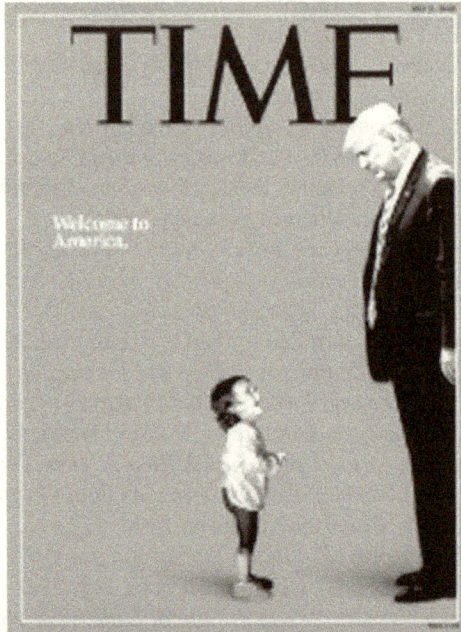

Government Protected Child Stealing – Next Generation

INDEX

About the Author - Then and Now

Lori Carangelo's 1963 Hamden Connecticut high school yearbook page predicted that she would have a career in Child Welfare. Instead, Lori devoted much of her life to opposing the corrupt Child Welfare System. In 1989, she founded Americans For Open Records (AmFOR), a nationwide network of volunteer "searchers" who, over the next 20 years, enabled thousands of adoptees to connect with their unknown biological families without fee. Many of the reunions were some of the first featured via television, radio, and newspapers, detailing the issues imposed on families touched by adoption. The information gleaned from the reunions was also utilized when she served as Data Source to the United Nations Rights of the Child Project and Sale For Adoption Report.

Born in 1945 to Italian-American parents in New Haven, Connecticut, Lori is retired from 25 years administration of environmental, job training/placement, and building departments in Santa Barbara and Palm Desert, California. She has authored over 600 published articles and 25 unique non-fiction books, including adoption-themed and "true crime" stories, to answer the often asked question as to *"why"* they did it and *how* to prevent negative outcomes that result from America's adoption, foster care, immigration and penal system laws, policies and practices.

More Books by Lori Carangelo

SCHOOL SHOOTERS
Why They Did It and America's War on Guns

THE ULTIMATE SEARCH BOOK – U.S. & World Editions
Adoption, Genealogy & Other Search Secrets

THE ADOPTION AND DONOR CONCEPTION FACTBOOK
The Only Comprehensive Source of U.S. & Global Data

CHOSEN CHILDREN
*Children As Commodities in America's Foster Care,
Adoption and Immigration Systems*

ADOPTION UNCENSORED
4 Decades of Politics, People and Commentary

ADOPTED KILLERS
430 Adoptees Who Killed – How and Why They Did It

BLOOD RELATIVES
A True Story of Family Secrets and Murders

ESPOSITO
The First Mafioso

KONDRO
The "Uncle Joe" Killer

JAMES MUNRO –
And the Freeway Killers

EYEWITNESS
The Case of the Carefully Crafted Central Coast Rapist

SERIAL KILLERS ON THE INTERSTATE
200 Highway Killers by State

RAGE!
How an Adoption Ignited a Fire